STAR WARS™

Knitting the Galaxy

STAR WARS™

Knitting the Galaxy

The Official *Star Wars* Knitting Pattern Book

TANIS GRAY

PAVILION

INSIGHT EDITIONS

San Rafael • Los Angeles • London

CONTENTS

Project Skill Levels

/ BEGINNER

// INTERMEDIATE

/// ADVANCED

INTRODUCTION

From its first appearance on the silver screen in 1977, *Star Wars* was an instant classic. People loved the characters, the creatures, the glimpses of planets beyond our own galaxy and the classic tale of good versus evil. Acclaimed for its groundbreaking special effects, the film uses cutting-edge technology, models, moviemaking illusions, puppets and more to create a universe where people fly around in spaceships, droids are commonplace and the light side and the dark side create balance. For the first time in cinematic history, people lined up for blocks to see a science-fiction movie, and for five years, it was the highest-grossing film at the box office. George Lucas and his group of rebels took the world – adults and children alike – by storm.

Knitters have long created *Star Wars*–themed garments inspired by fibretastic fandom. In many ways, being a knitter is like being a Jedi: we use our crafty powers for good, instruct apprentices in the way of the Fibre, concentrate and let the magic flow through our fingers – albeit into our needles, not our lightsabers. With a collection of projects including costume replicas, inspired-by garments, home decor and cuddly creatures, this is the first official book of *Star Wars* knitting patterns, representing selections from the nine main films of the *Star Wars* saga. Whether you're Jedi or Sith, a new fan or a longtime enthusiast, there is a project here for you: a pullover inspired by Darth Vader's chest piece (page 165), a set of droid scatter cushions (page 189), a pocket-sized Yoda toy (page 17) and much, much more.

The patterns include a wide range of techniques from cabling to stranded colourwork and double knitting to beading, as well as a wide range of sizes for both kids and adults. Each project is rated according to difficulty level and includes all the information you need to knit it. For a little extra inspiration, quotes, film stills and behind-the-scenes trivia are sprinkled throughout the book, allowing readers to truly immerse themselves in the galaxy of *Star Wars*.

On behalf of the incredibly talented designers from across the globe whose creative prowess has brought this beloved film saga to life through yarn and needle, I am delighted to celebrate these wonderful characters and stories with you, my fellow *Star Wars*–loving knitters.

May the Force be with you.

Tanis

TOYS

'A LONG TIME AGO, IN A
GALAXY FAR, FAR AWAY....'

—*STAR WARS*: EPISODE IV *A NEW HOPE*

PORG

Designed by: **SUSAN CLAUDINO**

LEVEL: //

The sequel trilogy introduces fans to many exciting new characters and creatures in the *Star Wars* universe: Rey, Poe, Finn, BB-8 and, of course, porgs. Residents of the sacred Jedi island on Ahch-To, these puffin-like birds are under 30 cm (12 in.) tall and covered in feathers, with large webbed feet, huge eyes and no beak. They have the ability to both swim and fly, and in one memorable scene, serve as dinner for a hungry Chewbacca.

Porgs were a big hit with fans of all ages, and now you can knit one of your very own. For minimal finishing, the porg's body, wings, tail, legs and feet are worked in the round using the Magic Loop method. The belly patch is worked flat, so it can be attached to the body as it is firmly stuffed. The wings, tail and legs are sewn on at the end, while locking safety eyes ensure that this porg is a safe playmate for little fans.

SIZE
One size

FINISHED MEASUREMENTS
Width: 11.5 cm / 4½ in.
Height: 11 cm / 4¼ in.

YARN
Aran weight (medium #4) yarn, shown in Plymouth Yarn *Galway Worsted* (100% wool; 192 m / 210 yd per 100 g / 3½ oz skein)
Colour A: #759 Reese Cup, 1 skein
Colour B: #8 Bleach, 1 skein
Colour C: #91 Clementine Orange, 1 skein

NEEDLES
• 3.75 mm/US 5 set of 4 or 5 double-pointed needles

NOTIONS
• Stitch marker
• Waste yarn
• Tapestry needle
• Two 15 mm/ ⅝ in. black safety eyes
• Small piece of white craft felt
• 45 cm / 18 in. length of grey embroidery thread
• Polyester stuffing

TENSION
23 sts and 28 rnds = 10 cm / 4 in. in St st
Tension is not critical for a toy; just ensure the stitches are tight enough so the stuffing will not show through your finished project.

Continued on page 12

PATTERN STITCH

Stocking Stitch (any number of sts)

Row 1 (RS): Knit.

Row 2 (WS): Purl.

Rep Rows 1 and 2 for patt.

Worked in the rnd: Knit all rnds.

NOTES

- All pieces for this toy are worked separately, then sewn together. The body, wings, tail, legs and feet are all worked in the round for minimal finishing. The white belly patch is knit flat. The eyes are attached before stuffing.

BELLY PATCH

With colour B, CO 20 sts, leaving a 45 cm / 18 in. tail.

Row 1 (WS): Purl.

Row 2 (RS, inc): K1, k1f&b, k16, k1f&b, k1 – 22 sts.

Rows 3–5: Cont in St st, work 3 rows even.

Row 6 (inc): K1, k1f&b, k18, k1f&b, k1 – 24 sts.

Rows 7–15: Work even.

Row 16 (dec): K1, ssk, k18, k2tog, k1 – 22 sts rem.

Row 17: Purl.

Row 18 (dec): K1, ssk, k16, k2tog, k1 – 20 sts rem.

Row 19: Purl.

Row 20 (dec): K1, ssk, k14, k2tog, k1 – 18 sts rem.

Row 21: Purl.

Row 22 (dec): K1, ssk, k12, k2tog, k1 – 16 sts rem.

Row 23: Purl.

Row 24 (dec): K1, ssk, k10, k2tog, k1 – 14 sts rem.

Row 25: Purl.

Row 26 (dec): K1, ssk, k8, k2tog, k1 – 12 sts rem.

Row 27: Purl.

Row 28 (dec): K1, ssk, k6, k2tog, k1 – 10 sts rem.

Row 29: Purl.

Row 30 (dec): *K2tog; rep from * to end of row – 5 sts rem.

Row 31: Purl.

Row 32 (dec): K1, s2kp, k1 – 3 sts rem.

Cut yarn and thread through rem 3 sts.

BODY

With colour A, CO 4 sts. Pm and join to work in the rnd, being careful not to twist sts.

Rnd 1 (inc): *K1f&b; rep from * to end of rnd – 8 sts.

Rnd 2 (inc): *K1f&b; rep from * to end of rnd – 16 sts.

Rnd 3 (inc): *K1, k1f&b; rep from * to end of rnd – 24 sts.

Rnd 4 (inc): *K2, k1f&b; rep from * to end of rnd – 32 sts.

Rnd 5 (inc): *K3, k1f&b; rep from * to end of rnd – 40 sts.

Rnd 6 (inc): *K4, k1f&b; rep from * to end of rnd – 48 sts.

Rnd 7 (inc): *K5, k1f&b; rep from * to end of rnd – 56 sts.

Rnd 8 (inc): *K6, k1f&b; rep from * to end of rnd – 64 sts.

Rnd 9 (inc): *K7, k1f&b; rep from * to end of rnd – 72 sts.

Rnds 10–34: Knit.

Rnd 35 (dec): *K4, k2tog; rep from * to end of rnd – 60 sts rem.

Rnd 36: Knit.

Rnd 37 (dec): *K3, k2tog; rep from * to end of rnd – 48 sts rem.

Rnd 38: Knit.

Rnd 39 (dec): *K2, k2tog; rep from * to end of rnd – 36 sts rem.

Rnd 40: Knit.

Rnd 41 (dec): *K1, k2tog; rep from * to end of rnd – 24 sts rem.

Rnd 42: Knit.

Lightly stuff body.

Using long CO tail, sew belly patch to body just above last inc rnd, stretching bottom edge slightly if necessary to fit between first and fourth inc on front.

EYES

Cut out 2 circles from felt, using the washer from the safety eyes as patt. Mark position for the post of safety eye in centre of each circle. Snip a small *X* in the felt and push safety eye post through the snip. Using photos as a guide, insert each safety eye into head through both layers and secure with washer on inside of body.

Add more stuffing, and cont to stuff as needed.

Rnd 43 (dec): *K2tog; rep from * to end of rnd – 12 sts rem.

Rnd 44 (dec): *K2tog; rep from * to end of rnd – 6 sts rem.

Cut yarn, leaving a long tail. Thread through rem sts and pull tight to close hole, then pull tail to inside.

WINGS (MAKE 2)

With colour A, CO 8 sts, leaving a long tail. Pm and join to work in the rnd, being careful not to twist sts.

Rnds 1–2: Knit.

Rnd 3 (inc): *K1, (k1f&b) twice, k1; rep from * once more – 12 sts.

Rnds 4–7: Knit.

Rnd 8 (inc): K1, (k1f&b, k2) 3 times, k1f&b, k1 – 16 sts.

Rnd 9: Knit.

Rnd 10 (inc): *K1, k1f&b, k4, k1f&b, k1; rep from * once more – 20 sts.

Rnd 11: Knit.

Rnd 12 (inc): *K1, k1f&b, k6, k1f&b, k1; rep from * once more – 24 sts.

Rnds 13–18: Knit.

Rnd 19 (dec): K1, ssk, k18, k2tog, k1 – 22 sts rem.

Rnd 20 (dec): K1, ssk, k16, k2tog, k1 – 20 sts rem.

Rnd 21 (dec): K1, ssk, k14, k2tog, k1 – 18 sts rem.

Rnd 22 (dec): K1, ssk, k12, k2tog, k1 – 16 sts rem.

Rnd 23 (dec): K1, ssk, k10, k2tog, k1 – 14 sts rem.

Rnd 24 (dec): K1, ssk, k8, k2tog, k1 – 12 sts rem.

Rnd 25 (dec): K1, ssk, k6, k2tog, k1 – 10 sts rem.

Rnd 26 (dec): K1, ssk, k4, k2tog, k1 – 8 sts rem.

Rnd 27 (dec): K1, ssk, k2, k2tog, k1 – 6 sts rem.

Rnd 28 (dec): K1, ssk, k2tog, k1 – 4 sts rem.

Rnd 29: Knit.

Rnd 30 (dec): Ssk, k2tog – 2 sts rem.

Cut yarn and thread tail through rem sts.

TAIL

With colour A, CO 4 sts. Pm and join to work in the rnd, being careful not to twist sts.

Rnd 1: Knit.

Rnd 2 (inc): *K1f&b; rep from * to end of rnd – 8 sts.

Rnds 3–4: Knit.

BEHIND THE SCENES:

Porgs were not in the original script for *The Last Jedi*. They were added by writer-director Rian Johnson after discovering that the island of Skellig Michael — where the Ahch-To scenes were shot — was crawling with puffins. Johnson came up with the idea of digitally replacing the puffins with a new species that blends the characteristics of a pug and a seal through a combination of CGI, animatronics and puppetry. And so, porgs were born.

'WHEN DID THIS OLD RATTLETRAP BECOME A BIRDCAGE?'

–GENERAL LEIA ORGANA, *STAR WARS*: EPISODE VIII *THE LAST JEDI* (NOVELISATION)

Rnd 5 (inc): *K1, (k1f&b) twice, k2, (k1f&b) twice, k1 – 12 sts.

Rnds 6–7: Knit.

Rnd 8 (inc): K1, (k1f&b, k2) 3 times, k1f&b, k1 – 16 sts.

Rnds 9–10: Knit.

Cast off, leaving a 25 cm/10 in. long tail.

LEGS AND FEET (MAKE 2)

LEG

With colour C, CO 4 sts, leaving a 25 cm / 10 in. tail. Pm and join to work in the rnd, being careful not to twist sts.

Rnds 1–12: Knit.

FOOT

Rnd 13 (inc): *K1f&b; rep from * to end of rnd – 8 sts.

Rnd 14 (inc): *K1, (k1f&b) twice, k2, (k1f&b) twice, k1 – 12 sts.

Rnds 15–17: Knit.

TOES

Rnd 18: K2, slip next 8 sts to waste yarn, k2 – 4 sts rem. Join to work in the rnd.

Rnd 19: Knit.

Rnd 20 (dec): (Ssk) twice – 2 sts rem.

Cut yarn and thread through rem sts. Pull tight to close hole, then pull tail to inside.

Return first 2 sts and last 2 sts from waste yarn to needles, leaving rem 4 sts on waste yarn – 4 sts.

Join colour C, leaving a tail to close hole between toes. Rep Rnds 18–20 for 2nd toe.

Cut yarn and thread tail through rem sts. Pull tight to close hole, then pull tail to inside.

Return rem 4 sts to needle. Join colour C, leaving a tail to close hole between toes. Rep Rnds 18–20 for 3rd toe.

Cut yarn and thread tail through rem sts. Pull tight to close hole, then pull tail to inside.

FINISHING

Sew legs to lower body just below each corner of belly patch. Refer to photos to help with placement.

Sew tail to centre of lower back just above last inc rnd.

Sew wings to sides of body next to beg of dec on belly patch.

Use grey embroidery thread to add facial features, using straight lines for mouth and nostrils. Refer to photos to help with stitch placement.

BEHIND THE SCENES:

The porgs' cries were a mixture of the calls of turkeys, doves and chickens.

POCKET YODA

Designed by: **SUSAN CLAUDINO**

LEVEL: ///

The wisest of all Jedi, Yoda trains young Padawans in the ways of the Force until he is driven into exile by Emperor Palpatine in *Star Wars*: Episode III *Revenge of the Sith*. Having witnessed both the rise and fall of the Republic, Yoda flees to the swampy planet of Dagobah, where he studies the living Force and learns how to use its secrets after death. Endowed with immortality, he continues to offer advice to Luke when he needs it most.

Want to keep the advice of the Jedi Master right in your pocket? Now you can! The head and body are knit in the round in one continuous piece using the Magic Loop method, and the ears, limbs and cane are also worked in the round for minimal finishing. Yoda's robe is worked flat back and forth, with stitches cast off for the armholes, then later picked up around the opening and knit to form sleeves. Purl marks are added for easy placement of his ears, eyes and arms, allowing this pocket version of the 900-year-old Jedi to come together with minimal fuss.

SIZE
One size

FINISHED MEASUREMENTS
Width: approx 7 cm / 2¾ in., not including ears
Height: approx **11.5 cm** / 4½ in.

YARN
Aran weight (medium #4) yarn, shown in Plymouth Yarn *Galway Worsted* (100% wool; 192 m / 210 yd per 100 g / 3½ oz skein)
Colour A: #176 Endive Green, 1 skein
Colour B: #208 Walnut, 1 skein
Colour C: #722 Sand Heather, 1 skein

NEEDLES
- 3.75 mm / US 5, 100 cm / 40 in. long circular needle, or set of 4 or 5 double-pointed needles

NOTIONS
- Stitch marker
- Waste yarn
- Tapestry needle
- Two 12 mm / ½ in. green safety eyes
- Polyester stuffing
- Wood toothpick (for cane, optional)
- Removeable stitch marker or safety pin (optional)

TENSION
23 sts and 28 rnds = 10 cm / 4 in. in St st
Tension is not critical for a toy; just ensure the stitches are tight enough so the stuffing will not show through your finished project.

CONTINUED ON PAGE 18

BODY

With colour B, CO 4 sts. Pm and join to work in the rnd, being careful not to twist sts.

Rnd 1 (inc): *K1f&b; rep from * to end of rnd – 8 sts.

Rnd 2 (inc): *K1, k1f&b; rep from * to end of rnd – 12 sts.

Rnd 3 (inc): *K2, k1f&b; rep from * to end of rnd – 16 sts.

Rnd 4 (inc): *K3, k1f&b; rep from * to end of rnd – 20 sts.

Rnd 5 (inc): *K4, k1f&b; rep from * to end of rnd – 24 sts.

Rnds 6–8: Knit.

Rnd 9 (dec): *Ssk, k10; rep from * once more – 22 sts rem.

Rnd 10 (dec): *K9, k2tog; rep from * once more – 20 sts rem.

Rnd 11: Knit.

Rnd 12 (dec): *Ssk, k8; rep from * once more – 18 sts rem.

Rnd 13 (dec): *K7, k2tog; rep from * once more – 16 sts rem.

Rnd 14: Knit.

Rnd 15 (dec): *Ssk, k4, k2tog; rep from * once more – 12 sts rem.

Rnd 16: P1 for arm placement, k4, p2 for arm placement, k4, p1 for arm placement.

Rnd 17: Knit.

Stuff body.

Rnd 18: Purl.

Cut colour B and join colour A.

HEAD

Rnd 19 (inc): *K1f&b; rep from * to end of rnd – 24 sts.

Rnd 20 (inc): *K1f&b; rep from * to end of rnd – 48 sts.

Rnds 21–25: Knit.

Rnd 26: K25, p1 for ear placement, k20, p1 for ear placement, k1.

Rnd 27: K8, p1 for eye placement, k6, p1 for eye placement, knit to end of rnd.

Rnd 28: Knit.

Rnd 29: K25, p1 for ear placement, k20, p1 for ear placement, k1.

Rnds 30–34: Knit.

Rnd 35 (dec): *K6, k2tog; rep from * to end of rnd – 42 sts rem.

Rnd 36 (dec): *K5, k2tog; rep from * to end of rnd – 36 sts rem.

Rnd 37 (dec): *K4, k2tog; rep from * to end of rnd – 30 sts rem.

Rnd 38 (dec): *K3, k2tog; rep from * to end of rnd – 24 sts rem.

Insert safety eyes at purl sts on Rnd 27 according to package instructions.

Stuff head and cont stuffing as needed.

Rnd 39 (dec): *K2, k2tog; rep from * to end of rnd – 18 sts rem.

Rnd 40 (dec): *K1, k2tog; rep from * to end of rnd – 12 sts rem.

Rnd 41 (dec): *K2tog; rep from * to end of rnd – 6 sts rem.

Cut yarn, leaving a long tail. Thread tail through rem sts and pull tight to close hole, then pull tail to inside.

Weave in ends.

'SIZE MATTERS NOT. LOOK AT ME. JUDGE ME BY MY SIZE, DO YOU? HM? HM. AND WELL YOU SHOULD NOT, FOR MY ALLY IS THE FORCE, AND A POWERFUL ALLY IT IS.'

–YODA, *STAR WARS*: EPISODE V *THE EMPIRE STRIKES BACK*

EARS (MAKE 2)

With colour A, CO 12 sts, leaving a long tail. Pm and join to work in the rnd, being careful not to twist sts.

Rnds 1–2: Knit.

Rnd 3 (dec): K1, ssk, k6, k2tog, k1– 10 sts rem.

Rnd 4 (dec): K1, ssk, k4, k2tog, k1 – 8 sts rem.

Rnds 5–8: Knit.

Rnd 9 (dec): K1, ssk, k2, k2tog, k1 – 6 sts rem.

Rnd 10 (dec): K1, ssk, k2tog, k1 – 4 sts rem.

Rnd 11 (dec): Ssk, k2tog – 2 sts rem.

Rnd 12: Knit.

Cut yarn. Thread tail through rem sts and pull tight to close hole, then pull tail to inside.

Weave in ends.

FEET (MAKE 2)

With colour A, CO 6 sts, leaving a long tail. Pm and join to work in the rnd, being careful not to twist sts.

Rnds 1–3: Knit.

FIRST TOE

Row 1 (RS): K2, turn, leaving rem 4 sts unworked.

Row 2 (WS): P2, turn.

Row 3 (dec): K2tog – 1 st rem.

Cut yarn and pull through rem st.

SECOND TOE

Rejoin colour A to rem sts.

Row 1 (RS): K2, turn, leaving rem 2 sts unworked.

Row 2 (WS): P2, turn.

Row 3 (dec): K2tog – 1 st rem.

Cut yarn and pull through rem st.

THIRD TOE

Rejoin colour A to rem sts.

Row 1 (RS): K2.

Row 2 (WS): P2.

Row 3 (dec): K2tog – 1 st rem.

Cut yarn and pull through rem st.

Weave in ends.

ARMS (MAKE 2)

With colour B, CO 6 sts, leaving a long tail. Pm and join to work in the rnd, being careful not to twist sts.

Rnds 1–12: Knit.

Cut colour B and join colour A.

HAND

Rnds 13–14: Knit.

FIRST FINGER

Rnd 15: K1, slip next 4 sts to waste yarn, k1 – 2 sts rem.

Rnd 16: Knit.

Cut yarn and pull tail through sts to fasten off.

SECOND FINGER

Return first st and last st from waste yarn to needle, leaving rem 2 sts on waste yarn – 2 sts.

Join colour B. Knit 2 rnds.

Cut yarn and pull tail through sts to fasten off.

THIRD FINGER

Return rem 2 sts to needle.

Join colour B. Knit 2 rnds.

Cut yarn and pull tail through sts to fasten off.

Weave in ends.

ROBE
BODY

With colour C, CO 24 sts. Do not join.

Row 1 (WS): Knit.

DIVIDE FOR ARMHOLES

Row 2 (RS): K4, cast off 3 sts for armhole, k9 more sts, cast off 3 sts for armhole, k3 more sts – 18 sts rem, with 4 sts for each front and 10 sts for back.

LOWER BODY

Row 3: K2, p2, CO 3 sts using Backward Loop method, p10, CO 3 sts, p2, k2 – 24 sts.

Row 4: Knit.

Row 5: K2, p20, k2.

Rows 6–13: Rep Rows 4–5 four more times.

Row 14: Knit.

Cast off all sts loosely kwise.

SLEEVES

With colour C and RS facing, pick up and knit 3 sts in armhole cast-off edge, 1 st in gap, 3 sts in CO edge at top of armhole, then 1 st in gap – 8 sts. Pm and join to work in the rnd.

Knit 9 rnds.

Cast off sts.

Weave in ends.

CANE

With colour B, CO 3 sts.

Row 1: K3, but do not turn. Slide sts back to right end of needle.

Row 2: Pull yarn across back of work, k3, but do not turn. Slide sts back to right end of needle.

Rep last row 7 more times.

Cut yarn. Thread tail through sts and pull tight to close hole, then pull tail to inside.

Insert a wood toothpick in centre of i-cord, then cut to fit.

FINISHING

Sew feet to bottom of the body.

Sew arms to sides of body at purl sts on Rnd 16.

Sew ears to side of head at purl sts on Rnds 26 and 29, making sure to completely cover purl sts.

Carefully pull arms through sleeves of robe. *Note:* If hands are difficult to pull through, try using a removable stitch marker or safety pin inserted in the fingers to gently guide them through the sleeves.

Using colour A, sew cane to hands with a few sts.

Using colour A and straight sts, add facial features. Refer to the photos to help with placement. The nose is created by working several short straight sts on top of each other.

CHEWIE

Designed by: **SUSAN CLAUDINO**

LEVEL: ///

Han Solo's faithful friend and co-pilot of the *Millennium Falcon*, Chewbacca is one of the most beloved and consistent characters in the *Star Wars* films, appearing in all three major trilogies. Chewbacca is a Wookiee: extraordinarily tall, strong and intelligent, covered in brown and caramel-coloured fur. His only accessories are a bandolier, carry pouch and bowcaster. Like most Wookiees, Chewie is willing to put his life on the line for friendship and honour. He is loyal to his co-pilot until the end and carries on with their mission long after Han Solo's death in *The Force Awakens*.

This cuddly Chewie is knit in the round from the bottom up for minimal finishing and stuffed as you go. The feet and legs are worked first, then joined together with additional cast-on stitches for the body and head. Eyes, nose and arms placement are all marked with purl bumps to ensure proper positioning. The bag portion of the bandolier is knit in the round, with half the stitches cast off and the remaining stitches worked flat to create the flap. The strap is knit flat in two colours, with the yarns carried up the side. Simple straight stitching creates a mouth. After completion, the yarn is brushed vigorously to create a fuzzier appearance.

SIZE
One size

FINISHED MEASUREMENT
Height: 29 cm / 11½ in.

YARN
Colour A: 4-ply weight (fine #2) yarn, shown in Rowan *Kidsilk Haze* (70% mohair, 30% silk; 210 m / 230 yd per 25 g / .88 oz ball), in colour #00686 Lustre, 1 ball

Colour B: DK weight (light #3) yarn, shown in Rowan *Alpaca Classic* (57% alpaca, 43% cotton; 120 m / 131 yd per 25 g / .88 oz ball), in colour #00114 Golden Girl, 1 ball

Colour C: Aran weight (medium #4) yarn, shown in Plymouth Yarn *Galway Worsted* (100% wool; 192 m / 210 yd per 100 g / 3½ oz skein), in colour #759 Reese Cup, 1 skein

Colour D: Aran weight (medium #4) yarn, shown in Plymouth Yarn *Encore Starz* (74% acrylic, 25% wool, 1% polyester; 183 m / 200 yd per 100 g / 3½ oz skein), in colour #G194 Medium Grey, 1 skein

NEEDLES
- 3.25 mm / US 3, 100 cm / 40 in. long circular needle for Magic Loop method, set of 4 or 5 double-pointed needles

NOTIONS
- Stitch marker
- Waste yarn or stitch holders
- Tapestry needle
- Two 15 mm / ⅝ in. black safety eyes
- One 15 mm / ⅝ in. black oval safety nose
- Polyester stuffing
- Brush or comb to create fur/fluff

CONTINUED ON PAGE 24

TENSION

30 sts and 33 rnds = 10 cm / 4 in. in St st with 2 strands of colour A held together or 1 strand of colour B

Tension is not critical for a toy; just ensure the stitches are tight enough so the stuffing will not show through your finished project.

SPECIAL TECHNIQUE
JUDY'S MAGIC CAST ON

Leaving a tail about 2.5 cm / 1 in. long for each stitch to be cast on, lay the yarn over the first needle, with the tail in front and the end coming from the ball at the back of the needle. Hold the second needle parallel below the first needle and over the tail.

Move the tail to the back and move the end from the ball to the front below the needles, in front of the tail yarn; this forms the first stitch on the top needle. Insert thumb and index finger between the strands and spread them apart as you would for a long tail cast on. Continue holding both needles parallel as you cast on, and work with the needles as a single unit while wrapping the yarn ends around and between both needles.

1. Bring the lower needle over the top of the index finger yarn. Move the index finger yarn up in front of the lower needle, then down between the needles to cast on one stitch on the lower needle.

2. Point both needles downwards. Taking the bottom needle over the top of the thumb yarn, bring the thumb yarn up between the needles, then over the top of the top needle. Return both needles to horizontal position to cast on one stitch on the top needle.

Repeat steps 1 and 2 until you have the required number of stitches on both needles.

Remove your thumb and index finger from the yarn ends. Turn the needles so the tails are on the right and the bottom needle is now on top; the last stitch cast on should be the first stitch on the top. Because the yarns are not anchored on the needle, twist both tails around each other to secure the stitches.

To begin knitting using the Magic Loop method, pull the lower needle tip and cable through the cast-on stitches, keeping both sets of stitches separated by a length of the cable as for a regular round of Magic Loop knitting. Knit the stitches on the top needle. Rotate the needles so that the stiches just worked are on the bottom, pull the lower needle tip through the stitches and work the stitches on the top needle.

If you're working with double-pointed needles, use a third needle to knit the stitches on the top needle. Rotate the needles so that the stitches just worked are on the bottom, then with the third needle knit the stitches on the top needle.

NOTES

- When working with Colour A, hold two strands of yarn together using the ends from the centre and outside of the ball. All other colors are knit with only one strand of yarn.

- All pieces are knit in the round for minimal finishing, except the bandolier strap and bag flap, which are knit flat.

- The legs are worked separately, then joined to knit the body and head, stuffing as you go. Purl stitches mark the placement of the eyes, nose and arms. The arms are worked separately and stuffed as you go, then sewn to the body.

- The bag is knit in the round from the bottom up using a Judy's Magic Cast On, then the flap is worked back and forth over half the stitches after casting off the other half of the stitches.

- Slip stitches purlwise with the yarn held at the back unless instructed otherwise.

LEGS (MAKE 2)
FOOT
With colour A, CO 4 sts. Pm and join to work in the rnd, being careful not to twist sts.

Rnd 1 (inc): *K1f&b; rep from * to end of rnd – 8 sts.

Rnd 2 (inc): *K1f&b; rep from * to end of rnd – 16 sts.

Rnd 3 (inc): *K1, k1f&b; rep from * to end of rnd – 24 sts.

Rnd 4 (inc): *K2, k1f&b; rep from * to end of rnd – 32 sts.

Rnd 5 (inc): *K3, k1f&b; rep from * to end of rnd – 40 sts.

Rnd 6 (inc): *K4, k1f&b; rep from * to end of rnd –48 sts.

Rnd 7: Knit.

Cut colour A and join colour B.

Rnds 8–10: Knit.

Rnd 11 (dec): K8, (k3tog) 3 times, k31 – 42 sts rem.

Rnd 12: Knit.

Rnd 13 (dec): K8, k3tog, k31 – 40 sts rem.

Rnds 14–16: Knit.

LEG

Rnd 17 (dec): K16, ssk, k20, k2tog –38 sts rem.

Rnd 18: Knit.

Rnd 19 (dec): K16, ssk, k18, k2tog – 36 sts rem.

Rnd 20: Knit.

Rnd 21 (dec): K16, ssk, k16, k2tog – 34 sts rem.

Rnd 22: Knit.

Rnd 23 (dec): K16, ssk, k14, k2tog – 32 sts rem.

Rnds 24–26: Knit.

Cut colour B and join colour A.

Rnds 27–28: K3, (sl 1, k4) twice, sl 1, k6, sl 1, k3, sl 1, k2, sl 1, k4.

Rnds 29–36: Knit.

Cut yarn and stuff leg. Place sts on holder or waste yarn.

'IT'S NOT WISE TO UPSET A WOOKIEE.'

—HAN SOLO, *STAR WARS*: EPISODE IV *A NEW HOPE*

Rep for second leg, but *do not cut yarn*.

JOIN LEGS

Rnd 37: Knit 16 sts of second leg, CO 8 sts using Backward Loop method, return 32 sts of first leg to needle, k32, CO 8 sts, then knit rem 16 sts of second leg –80 sts. Pm for beg of rnd.

BODY

Rnds 38–40: Knit.

Cut colour A and join colour B.

Rnds 43–44: *K5, sl 1, k2, sl 1, k1, sl 1, k3, sl 1, k2, sl 1, k6, sl 1, k2, sl 1, k3, sl 1, k1, sl 1, k4, sl 1, k1; rep from * once more.

Rnd 45: Knit.

Rnd 46 (dec): *Ssk, k38; rep from * once more – 78 sts rem.

Rnd 47 (dec): *K37, k2tog; rep from * once more – 76 sts rem.

Rnd 48: Knit.

Rnd 49 (dec): *Ssk, k36; rep from * once more –74 sts rem.

Rnd 50 (dec): *K35, k2tog; rep from * once more –72 sts rem.

Rnd 51: Knit.

Rnd 52 (dec): *Ssk, k34; rep from * once more – 70 sts rem.

Rnd 53 (dec): *K33, k2tog; rep from * once more –68 sts rem.

Rnd 54: Knit.

Rnd 55 (dec): *Ssk, k32; rep from * once more – 66 sts rem.

Rnd 56 (dec): *K31, k2tog; rep from * once more – 64 sts rem.

Rnd 57: Knit.

Rnd 58 (dec): *Ssk, k30; rep from * once more – 62 sts rem.

Rnd 59 (dec): *K29, k2tog; rep from * once more – 60 sts rem.

Rnd 60: Knit.

Rnd 61 (dec): *Ssk, k28; rep from * once more – 58 sts rem.

Rnd 62 (dec): *K27, k2tog; rep from * once more – 56 sts rem.

Rnd 63: Knit.

Rnd 64 (dec): *Ssk, k26; rep from * once more –54 sts rem.

Rnd 65 (dec): *K25, k2tog; rep from * once more – 52 sts rem.

Rnd 66: Knit.

Rnd 67 (dec): *Ssk, k24; rep from * once more – 50 sts rem.

Rnd 68 (dec): *K23, k2tog; rep from * once more – 48 sts rem.

Rnd 69: Knit.

Cut colour B and join colour A.

SHOULDERS AND NECK

Rnds 70–71: *K3, sl 1, k2, sl 1, k3, sl 1, k4, sl 1, k3, sl 1, k1, sl 1, k2; rep from * once more.

Rnd 72: Knit.

Sew tog CO edges between legs. Stuff body and cont stuffing as needed.

Rnds 73–75: Knit.

Rnd 76: P2 for arm placement, k20, p4 for arm placement, k20, p2 for arm placement.

Rnd 77: Knit.

Cut colour A and join colour B.

HEAD

Rnd 78 (inc): *K1f&b; rep from * to end of rnd – 96 sts.

Rnd 79 (inc): *K1f&b, k46, (k1f&b) twice, k46, k1f&b – 100 sts.

Rnds 80–83: Knit.

Rnd 84: K24, p2 for nose placement, k74.

Rnd 85: K19, p1 for eye placement, k10, p1 for eye placement, k69.

Rnds 86–89: Knit.

Cut colour B and join colour A.

Rnds 90–91: *K2, sl 1, k4, (sl 1, k2, sl 1, k3) twice, sl 1, k4, sl 1, k2, sl 1, k3, sl 1, k2, sl 1, k2, sl 1, k3, sl 1, k4, sl 1, k1; rep from * once more.

Rnds 92–101: Knit.

Rnd 102 (dec): *K8, k2tog; rep from * to end of rnd –90 sts rem.

Rnd 103: Knit.

Rnd 104 (dec): *K7, k2tog; rep from * to end of rnd –80 sts rem.

Rnd 105: Knit.

Rnd 106 (dec): *K6, k2tog; rep from * to end of rnd – 70 sts rem.

Rnd 107: Knit.

Rnd 108 (dec): *K5, k2tog; rep from * to end of rnd –60 sts rem.

Rnd 109: Knit.

Rnd 110 (dec): *K4, k2tog; rep from * to end of rnd – 50 sts rem.

Rnd 111: Knit.

Rnd 112 (dec): *K3, k2tog; rep from * to end of rnd – 40 sts rem.

Rnd 113: Knit.

Insert eyes and nose using purl sts for placement. Stuff head and cont stuffing as needed.

Rnd 114 (dec): *K2, k2tog; rep from * to end of rnd – 30 sts rem.

Rnd 115: Knit.

Rnd 116 (dec): *K1, k2tog; rep from * to end of rnd – 20 sts rem.

Rnd 117 (dec): *K2tog; rep from * to end of rnd – 10 sts rem.

Cut yarn, leaving a long tail. Thread tail through rem sts and pull tight to close hole, then pull tail to inside.

ARMS (MAKE 2)

With colour B, CO 4 sts. Pm and join to work in the rnd, being careful not to twist sts.

Rnd 1 (inc): *K1f&b; rep from * to end of rnd –8 sts.

Rnd 2 (inc): *K1, k1f&b; rep from * to end of rnd – 12 sts.

Rnd 3 (inc): *K2, k1f&b; rep from * to end of rnd – 16 sts.

Rnd 4 (inc): *K3, k1f&b; rep from * to end of rnd – 20 sts.

Rnd 5 (inc): *K4, k1f&b; rep from * to end of rnd –24 sts.

Rnd 6 (inc): *K5, k1f&b; rep from * to end of rnd – 28 sts.

Rnd 7 (inc): *K6, k1f&b; rep from * to end of rnd – 32 sts.

Rnds 8–13: Knit.

Rnd 14 (dec): *Ssk, k14; rep from * once more – 30 sts rem.

Rnd 15 (dec): *K13, k2tog; rep from * once more – 28 sts rem.

Rnd 16: Knit.

Rnd 17 (dec): *Ssk, k12; rep from * once more – 26 sts rem.

Rnd 18 (dec): *K11, k2tog; rep from * once more – 24 sts rem.

Rnd 19: Knit.

Stuff arm and cont stuffing as needed.

Rnd 20 (dec): *Ssk, k10; rep from * once more – 22 sts rem.

Rnd 21 (dec): *K9, k2tog; rep from * once more – 20 sts rem.

Rnd 22: Knit.

Rnd 23 (dec): *Ssk, k8; rep from * once more – 18 sts rem.

Rnd 24 (dec): *K7, k2tog; rep from * once more – 16 sts rem.

Rnd 25: Knit.

Rnd 26 (dec): *Ssk, k6; rep from * once more – 14 sts rem.

Rnd 27 (dec): *K5, k2tog; rep from * once more – 12 sts rem.

Rnds 28–30: Knit.

Cut colour B and join colour A.

Rnds 31–32: *K1, sl 1, k2, sl 1, k1; rep from * once more.

Rnds 33–41: Knit.

If working Magic Loop, make sure there are 6 sts on each end of needle; if working with dpns, distribute 6 sts each on 2 dpn. Join sts using Three-Needle Cast Off. Cut yarn, leaving a 25 cm / 10 in. tail.

BANDOLIER

BAG

With colour C, CO 16 sts using Judy's Magic Cast On, with 8 sts on each needle – 16 sts.

Rnd 1: Knit.

Rnd 2 (inc): *K1, k1f&b, k4, k1f&b, k1; rep from * once more – 20 sts.

Rnd 3: Knit.

Rnd 4 (inc): *K1, k1f&b, k6, k1f&b, k1; rep from * once more –24 sts.

Rnds 5–13: Knit.

Rnd 14: Cast off 12 sts, then knit to end of rnd – 12 sts rem.

FLAP

Row 1 (WS): Sl 1, p11.

Row 2 (RS, dec): Ssk, k8, k2tog – 10 sts rem.

Rows 3–5: Purl.

Row 6: Knit.

Rows 7–15: Rep Rows 5 and 6 four more times, then rep Row 5 again.

Row 16: Purl.

Cast off kwise.

STRAP

With colour C, pick up and knit 3 sts along one corner of bag at flap cast off.

Row 1 (WS): Purl.

Row 2 (RS): Knit.

Rows 3–7: Knit.

Join colour D. Carry unused colour loosely up side of work.

Rows 8–11: Knit with colour D.

Rows 12–13: Knit with colour C.

Rep Rows 8–13 thirteen more times, or until strap fits around the body, ending with colour C.

Cut colour D.

Knit 4 rows with colour C only.

Next row (RS): Knit.

Next row (WS): Purl.

Cast off sts kwise. Cut yarn, leaving a 25 cm / 10 in. tail. Weave in ends.

FINISHING

Sew arms to body at purl sts using yarn tails. Make sure pieces cover the purl bumps completely.

Using colour A and straight st embroidery, add eyelids and mouth. Refer to photos to help with placement.

To create fur, brush or comb vigorously up and down, then back and forth over the body, legs and arms.

Place bandolier with strap over left shoulder and under right arm.

DEATH STAR

Designed by: **CARISSA BROWNING**

LEVEL: //

Easily the most iconic space station in science fiction, the Death Star has become synonymous with villainy and authoritarianism. Designed by the Separatists and completed by the Empire, this massive weapon has the ability to wipe out entire planets. Its only design flaws are its inability to effectively track starfighters and its exposed thermal exhaust port, a 2-metre / 6-foot opening that links directly to its core.

Knit in shimmering metallic yarn, our Death Star is just as beautiful in its construction as the one on the big screen – though, fortunately, much less destructive. This toy is worked from the bottom (southern hemisphere) up and mostly in the round, with rapid increases that taper off as you approach the equator. In the northern hemisphere, stitches are cast off for the bottom of the laser dish hole, and the remaining stitches are worked back and forth. The laser dish is finished by casting on stitches over the hole and returning to working in the round. Once the north pole is closed, the sphere is blocked over an inflatable beach ball. Finally, stitches are picked up around the hole and the laser dish is worked inwards, adding stuffing as you work.

SIZE
One size

FINISHED MEASUREMENTS
Diameter: approx 25.5 cm / 14 in.
Circumference: approx 112 cm / 44 in.

YARN
Colour A: 2-ply weight (super fine #1) yarn, shown in Miss Babs *Yummy 2-Ply* (100% superwash merino wool; 400 yd. / 365 m per 110 g / 3.9 oz hank) in colour Ammo, 2 hanks
Colour B: 3-ply weight (super fine #1) yarn, shown in Miss Babs *Estrellita* (92% superwash merino wool, 8% lurex; 365 m / 400 yd per 115 g / 4 oz hank) in colour Ammo, 2 hanks

NEEDLES
- 3.5 mm / US 4, 40 cm / 16 in. long circular needle and set of 4 or 5 double-pointed needles or size needed to obtain correct tension

NOTIONS
- Stitch marker
- Tapestry needle
- Beach ball, approx 33 cm / 13 in. across when inflated
- One 900 g / 32 oz bag of polyester stuffing

TENSION
21 sts and 29 rnds = 10 cm / 4 in. in St st with both yarns held tog
Be sure to check your tension.

Continued on page 32

NOTES

- This toy is worked from the bottom up, in the round at first, then back and forth to form the laser dish hole, then rejoined to work in the round again. Once the top is closed, stitches are picked up around the hole and the laser dish is worked towards the centre.
- The entire bag of stuffing should be used to stuff your Death Star.
- One strand of each yarn is held together throughout.

SOUTHERN HEMISPHERE

With 1 strand each of colour A and colour B held tog, make a slipknot and place on dpn.

Next row: (K1, yo, k1) in slipknot – 3 sts. Do not turn; slide sts to right end of dpn.

Inc rnd 1: (K1f&b) 3 times – 6 sts. Distribute sts evenly over 3 dpn. Pm and join to work in the rnd.

Change to cir needle when necessary.

Inc rnd 2: *K1f&b; rep from * to end of rnd – 12 sts.

Knit 2 rnds even.

Inc rnd 3: *K1f&b; rep from * to end of rnd – 24 sts.

Knit 2 rnds even.

Inc rnd 4: *K1, k1f&b; rep from * to end of rnd –36 sts.

Knit 2 rnds even.

Inc rnd 5: *K1f&b, k2; rep from * to end of rnd – 48 sts.

Knit 2 rnds even.

Inc rnd 6: *K2, k1f&b, k1; rep from * to end of rnd – 60 sts.

Knit 2 rnds even.

Inc rnd 7: *K2, p1, k1, k1f&b; rep from * to end of rnd – 72 sts.

Next 2 rnds: *K2, p1; rep from * to end of rnd.

Inc rnd 8: *K1, k1f&b, p1, k2, p1; rep from * to end of rnd – 84 sts.

Next 2 rnds: *K2, p2, k2, p1; rep from * to end of rnd.

Inc rnd 9: *K2, p2, k1, k1f&b, p1; rep from * to end of rnd – 96 sts.

Next 2 rnds: *K2, p2; rep from * to end of rnd.

Inc rnd 10: *P2, k1, k1f&b, p2, k2; rep from * to end of rnd – 108 sts.

Next 3 rnds: *P2, k2, p3, k2; rep from * to end of rnd.

Inc rnd 11: *P2, k1, k1f&b, p3, k2; rep from * to end of rnd – 120 sts.

Next 3 rnds: *P2, k2, p4, k2; rep from * to end of rnd.

Inc rnd 12: *K1, k1f&b, p2, k4, p2; rep from * to end of rnd – 132 sts.

Next 3 rnds: *K2, p3, k4, p2; rep from * to end of rnd.

Inc rnd 13: *K1, k1f&b, p3, k4, p2; rep from * to end of rnd – 144 sts.

Next 3 rnds: *K2, p4, k4, p2; rep from * to end of rnd.

Inc rnd 14: *P2, k1, k1f&b, k2, p4, k2; rep from * to end of rnd – 156 sts.

Next 4 rnds: *P2, k2, p1, k2, p4, k2; rep from* to end of rnd.

Inc rnd 15: *P2, k1, k1f&b, p1, k2, p4, k2; rep from * to end of rnd – 168 sts.

Next 4 rnds: *(P2, k2) twice, p4, k2; rep from * to end of rnd.

Inc rnd 16: *(K2, p2) twice, k3, k1f&b, p2; rep from * to end of rnd – 180 sts.

Next 5 rnds: *(K2, p2) twice, k4, p3; rep from * to end of rnd.

Inc rnd 17: *(K2, p2) twice, k3, k1f&b, p3; rep from * to end of rnd – 192 sts.

Next 5 rnds: *(K2, p2) twice, k4, p4; rep from * to end of rnd.

Inc rnd 18: *P2, k1, k1f&b, p2, k2, p4, k4; rep from * to end of rnd – 204 sts.

Next 11 rnds: *P2, k2, p3, k2, p4, k4; rep from * to end of rnd.

EQUATOR

Purl 2 rnds.
Knit 1 rnd.
Purl 2 rnds.

NORTHERN HEMISPHERE

Next 4 rnds: *K4, p4, k2, p3, k2, p2; rep from * to end.

LASER DISH HOLE

Row 1 (RS): Cast off 10 sts, work in patt to last st, k1 – 194 sts rem.

Row 2 (WS, dec): Sl 1 wyif, k2tog, work to last 3 sts, k2tog, k1 – 2 sts dec'd.

Row 3 (dec): Sl 1 wyif, p2tog, work to last 3 sts, p2tog, k1 – 190 sts rem.

Row 4 (dec): Rep Row 2 – 188 sts rem.

Row 5: Sl 1 wyif, p1, work to last 2 sts, p1, k1.

Row 6 (dec): Rep Row 2 – 186 sts rem.

Row 7: Rep Row 5.

Row 8 (dec): Rep Row 2 – 184 sts rem.

Row 9 (dec): Sl 1 wyif, p5, k4, p2, *k2tog, k1, p2, k2, p4, k4, p2; rep from * to last 2 sts, p1, k1 – 174 sts rem.

Row 10: Sl 1 wyif, k1, work to last 2 sts, k2.

Row 11: Sl 1 wyif, p1, work to last 2 sts, p1, k1.

Rows 12–14: Rep Rows 10 and 11 once more, then rep Row 10 again.

Row 15 (dec): Sl 1 wyif, p4, k2tog, k3, p2, *k2, p2, k2, p3, k2tog, k3, p2; rep from * to last 2 sts, p1, k1 – 163 sts rem.

Rows 16–20: Rep Rows 10 and 11 twice more, then rep Row 10 once more.

Row 21 (dec): Sl 1 wyif, p1, k2tog, k1, p4, k2, *p2, k2, p2, k2tog, k1, p4, k2; rep from * to last 2 sts, p1, k1 – 152 sts rem.

Rows 22–24: Rep Rows 10 and 11 once more, then rep Row 10 again.

Row 25 (inc): Sl 1 wyif, p1, M1P, work to last 2 sts, M1P, p1, k1 – 154 sts.

Row 26 (dec): Sl 1 wyif, k2, p2, k4, p2, k2, *p1, p2tog, k1, p2, k4, p2, k2; rep from * to last st, k1 –144 sts rem.

BEHIND THE SCENES:

To make the Death Star, model makers used polystyrene, a material that began shrinking at the edges of the casting. This shrinking caused a gap between the two halves when fit together. George Lucas liked this gap and wrote it into the story line, creating a trench at the equator of the model for rebel fighters to fly through while attempting to shoot their blasters into the exhaust port.

'THAT'S NO MOON.
IT'S A SPACE STATION.'

—OBI-WAN KENOBI, *STAR WARS*: EPISODE IV *A NEW HOPE*

Row 27 (inc): Sl 1 wyif, p1, M1P, work to last 2 sts, M1L, p1, k1 – 146 sts.

Row 28: Sl 1 wyif, k1, work to last 2 sts, k2.

Row 29 (inc): Sl 1 wyif, p1, M1L, work to last 2 sts, M1L, p1, k1 – 148 sts.

Row 30 (inc): Sl 1 wyif, k1, M1L, work to last 2 sts, M1P, k2 – 150 sts.

Row 31 (dec): Sl 1 wyif, p3, *k2, p2, k4, p2, p2tog, p1; rep from * to last 3 sts, k1, p1, k1, cast off 5 sts – 144 sts rem.

Join to work in the rnd again.

Rnd 32: P4, k2, *p2, k4, p4, k2; rep from * to last 6 sts, pm for new beg of rnd.

Rnd 33: *P2, k4, p4, k2; rep from * to end of rnd.

Work 1 rnd even.

Change to dpn when necessary.

Dec rnd 1: *P2, k4, p3, k2tog, k1; rep from * to end of rnd – 132 sts rem.

Work 3 rnds even.

Dec rnd 2: *K2, p4, k2tog, k1, p2; rep from * to end of rnd – 120 sts rem.

Work 3 rnds even.

Dec rnd 3: *K2, p3, k2tog, k1, p2; rep from * to end of rnd – 108 sts rem.

Work 3 rnds even.

Dec rnd 4: *P2, k2tog, k1, p2, k2; rep from * to end of rnd – 96 sts rem.

Work 2 rnds even.

Dec rnd 5: *P1, k2tog, k1, p2, k2; rep from * to end of rnd – 84 sts rem.

Work 2 rnds even.

Dec rnd 6: *P1, k2, p1, k2tog, k1; rep from * to end of rnd – 72 sts rem.

Work 2 rnds even.

Dec rnd 7: *K2tog, k4; rep from * to end of rnd – 60 sts rem.

Knit 2 rnds even.

Dec rnd 8: *K2, k2tog, k1; rep from * to end of rnd – 48 sts rem.

Knit 2 rnds even.

Dec rnd 9: *K2tog, k2; rep from * to end of rnd – 36 sts rem.

Knit 2 rnds even.

Dec rnd 10: *K2tog, k1; rep from * to end of rnd – 24 sts rem.

Knit 2 rnds even.

Dec rnd 11: *K2tog; rep from * to end of rnd – 12 sts rem.

Dec rnd 12: *K2tog; rep from * to end of rnd – 6 sts rem.

Cut yarns, leaving long tails. Thread tails through rem sts and pull tight to close hole. Secure on WS.

FINISHING

Weave in ends.

Soak piece in cool water until thoroughly wet. Squeeze out excess water, making sure not to wring. Lay piece on towel and roll up towel. Squeeze again to remove more water.

Remove piece from towel. Insert deflated beach ball through laser dish hole and inflate. Allow to dry completely. Deflate beach ball and remove.

LASER DISH

With dpn, 1 strand each of colour A and colour B held tog, and with RS facing, pick up and knit 72 sts evenly around laser dish hole. Pm and join to work in the rnd.

Purl 1 rnd.

Knit 1 rnd.

Dec rnd 1: *K2tog, k4; rep from * to end of rnd – 60 sts rem.

Knit 2 rnds even.

Stuff piece until almost full.

Dec rnd 2: *K2, k2tog, k1; rep from * to end of rnd – 48 sts rem.

Knit 2 rnds even.

Dec rnd 3: *K2tog, k2; rep from * to end of rnd – 36 sts rem.

Knit 2 rnds even.

Finish stuffing piece firmly.

Dec rnd 4: *K2tog, k1; rep from * to end of rnd – 24 sts rem.

Knit 2 rnds even.

Dec rnd 5: *K2tog; rep from * to end of rnd – 12 sts rem.

Dec rnd 6: *K2tog; rep from * to end of rnd – 6 sts rem.

Cut yarns, leaving long tails. Thread tails through rem sts and pull tight to close hole. Secure tails and pull through to WS.

Weave in rem ends.

COSTUME
REPLICAS

'THE FORCE WILL BE WITH YOU.
ALWAYS.'

—OBI-WAN KENOBI, *STAR WARS*: EPISODE IV *A NEW HOPE*

LUKE SKYWALKER'S FLIGHT JACKET

Designed by: **MARTASCHMARTA**

LEVEL: ///

Growing up with his aunt and uncle on their moisture farm, Luke has always dreamed of becoming a pilot. He finally gets his chance at the end of *Star Wars*: Episode IV *A New Hope* when he joins the Rebel Starfleet in their attack on the Death Star. With many talented pilots flying X-wings equipped with droids, the Rebel Alliance is the first line of defence against the Empire and a force to be reckoned with in battle. The uniform worn by Luke and the other Alliance pilots in *A New Hope* is an undisputed classic: a bright orange flight suit, a helmet, a harness, thermal gloves, insulated boots, and a white flak jacket, worn to protect the upper torso.

Now, Luke's famous flak jacket can be part of your personal wardrobe. Versatile enough to be worn as a costume or an everyday accessory, this cropped jacket is a must-have for any fan. Knit in two identical pieces, the front and back of the flak jacket are trapezoidal-shaped, edged in attached i-cord, and joined by narrow straps going over the shoulders. The textured welting technique is done by picking up stitches from a previous row and three-needle joining as it is knit. An attached belt with belt loops creates a fitted look, cinching in at the waist.

SIZES

XS (S, M, L, XL, 2XL, 3XL, 4XL, 5XL)
Shown in size M.
Instructions are written for the
  smallest size, with larger sizes given
  in brackets; when only one number
  is given, it applies to all sizes.

FINISHED MEASUREMENTS

To fit Chest/Bust: 71–76 (81.5–86.5,
  91.5–96.5, 101.5–106.5, 112–117,
  122–127, 132–137, 142–147.5, 152.5–
  157.5) cm / 28–30 (32–34, 36–38,
  40–42, 44–46, 48–50, 52–54, 56–58,
  60–62) in.
Length: 44 (45, 45, 46.5, 47, 47.5,
  47.5, 49, 49) cm / 17¼ (17¾, 17¾,
  18¼, 18½, 18¾, 18¾, 19¼, 19¼) in.,
  including shoulder straps

YARN

Aran weight (medium #4) yarn, shown
  in Blue Sky Fibers *Woolstok Worsted*
  (100% fine Highland wool; 112 m
  / 123 yd per 50 g / 1¾ oz hank), in
  colour #1303 Highland Fleece, 6 (7,
  8, 9, 10, 11, 11, 12, 13) hanks

NEEDLES

- 5.5 mm / US 9, 60 cm / 24 in. long
  circular needle or size needed to
  obtain correct tension in St st
- 3.75 mm / US 5, 60 cm / 24 in. and
  80 cm / 32 in. or 100 cm / 40 in. long
  circular needle, and pair of straight
  or double-pointed needles (optional
  for belts and straps)

Continued on page 40

NOTIONS

- Locking stitch markers
- Tapestry needle
- One 40 mm / 1½ in. tri-glide slide buckle

TENSIONS

17½ sts and 27 rows = 10 cm / 4 in. in St st with larger needles

21 sts and 33 rows = 10 cm / 4 in. in St st with smaller needles

17½ sts and 55 rows = 10 cm / 4 in. in Welt patt with larger needles

Be sure to check your tensions.

PATTERN STITCHES

Welt Pattern (any number of sts)

Rows 1–6 for patt.

Row 1 (RS): Knit, and place locking marker on first st and last st of this row.

Rows 2 and 4 (WS): Purl.

Row 3: Knit.

Row 5: With shorter smaller cir needle and WS facing, pick up back of each st in Row 1, using markers as reference point. Remove markers. With RS facing and holding smaller needle behind larger needle, with larger cir needle, *knit tog 1 st from both needles; rep from * across row.

Row 6: Purl.

Rep Rows 1–6 for patt.

JACKET
FRONT

With larger cir needle, CO 50 (56, 66, 74, 82, 90, 98, 106, 114) sts. Do not join.

Next row (WS): Purl.

Work in Welt Patt for 21.5 (21.5, 20.5, 20.5, 19.5, 19, 18, 18, 16.5) cm / 8½ (8½, 8, 8, 7¾, 7½, 7, 7, 6½) in. from beg, ending with Row 5 of patt.

SHAPE ARMHOLES

Dec row (WS): P1, p2tog, purl to last 3 sts, sl 2 sts kwise 1 at a time, return sts to LH needle in turned position, p2tog-tbl, p1 – 2 sts dec'd.

Rep Dec row every 6 rows 7 (8, 9, 11, 12, 14, 15, 16, 18) more times – 34 (38, 46, 50, 56, 60, 66, 72, 76) sts rem.

Cont even until piece measures 33 (34.5, 34.5, 35.5, 36, 37, 37, 38, 38) cm / 13 (13½, 13½, 14, 14¼, 14½, 14½, 15, 15) in. from beg, ending with Row 6 of patt.

Next row (RS): Cast off loosely to end of row, but do not fasten off last st – 1 st rem.

I-CORD EDGING

Change to longer smaller cir needle.

With RS facing, sl rem st to RH needle, pm, work (yo, k1, yo) in corner st of edge, pm, pick up and knit 33 (36, 39, 42, 45, 45, 47, 50, 53) sts evenly along right armhole edge, 54 (56, 56, 58, 58, 60, 60, 62, 62) sts along right side edge, pm, (yo, k1, yo) in corner st, pm, pick up and knit 64 (80, 86, 95, 108, 118, 134, 140, 150) sts along CO edge, pm, (yo, k1, yo) in corner st, pm, pick up and knit 54 (56, 56, 58, 58, 60, 60, 62, 62) sts along left side edge, 33 (36, 39, 42, 45, 45, 47, 50, 53) sts along left armhole edge, pm, (yo, k1, yo) in corner st, pm, then pick up and knit 44 (49, 57, 65, 73, 78, 86, 96, 99) sts across top edge – 295 (326, 346, 373, 400, 419, 447, 473, 492) sts.

With RS facing, CO 8 sts using

Backward Loop method.

Row 1: K7, k2tog-tbl, return 8 sts to LH needle. Do not turn.

Remove marker.

TURN CORNER

Row 2: K8, return 8 sts to LH needle. Do not turn.

Row 3: K7, k2tog-tbl, return 8 sts to LH needle. Do not turn.

Rows 4–7: Rep Rows 2 and 3 twice more.

Remove marker.

STRAIGHT EDGE

Row 8: K7, k2tog-tbl, return 8 sts to LH needle. Do not turn.

Rep last row to marker. Remove marker.

Rep Rows 2–8 three more times. Graft rem 8 sts to CO edge.

BACK

Work same as front.

FINISHING

Weave in ends. Block to measurements.

BELT LOOPS (MAKE 2)

With smaller needles, CO 6 sts. Do not join.

Row 1 (RS): Sl 1 wyib, k3, sl 1 wyib, p1.

Row 2 (WS): Sl 1 wyib, p3, sl 1 wyif, p1.

Rep last 2 rows until piece measures 5 cm / 2 in. long.

Cast off all sts.

BELT
SHORT BELT END

With smaller needles, CO 8 sts. Do not join.

Row 1 (RS): Sl 1 wyib, k5, sl 1 wyib, p1.

Row 2 (WS): Sl 1 wyib, p5, sl 1 wyif, p1.

Rep last 2 rows until piece measures 20.5 (23, 25.5, 28, 30.5, 33, 35.5, 38, 40.5) cm / 8 (9, 10, 11, 12, 13, 14, 15, 16) in. long.

Cast off all sts.

Slip one end through buckle and fold under approx 2.5 cm / 1 in. Sew neatly to WS.

LONG BELT END

Work same as Short Belt End until piece measures approx 35.5 (40.5, 45.5, 50.5, 56, 61, 66, 71, 76) cm / 14 (16, 18, 20, 22, 24, 26, 28, 30) in. long.
Cast off all sts.

SHOULDER STRAPS (MAKE 2)

Work same as Short End Belt until piece measures 15 cm / 6 in. long.
Cast off all sts.

Weave in ends. Block pieces.
Sew belt loops to back, placing bottom edges 7.5 (9, 10, 11.5, 12.5, 14, 15, 16.5, 18) cm / 3 (3½, 4, 4½, 5, 5½, 6, 6½, 7) in. from bottom edge and placing outer edges 10 (11, 12.5, 14, 16, 17, 19, 20.5, 22) cm / 4 (4¼, 5, 5½, 6¼, 6¾, 7½, 8, 8¾) in. from side edges.
Sew short belt end to left front and long belt end to right front, placing end of belt at pick-up edge of i-cord edging and 7.5 (9, 10, 11.5, 12.5, 14, 15, 16.5, 18) cm / 3 (3½, 4, 4½, 5, 5½, 6, 6½, 7) in. from bottom edge.
Sew end of each shoulder strap to each side of front and back, with outer edges even with i-cord edging and short ends of straps even with pick-up edge of i-cord edging.

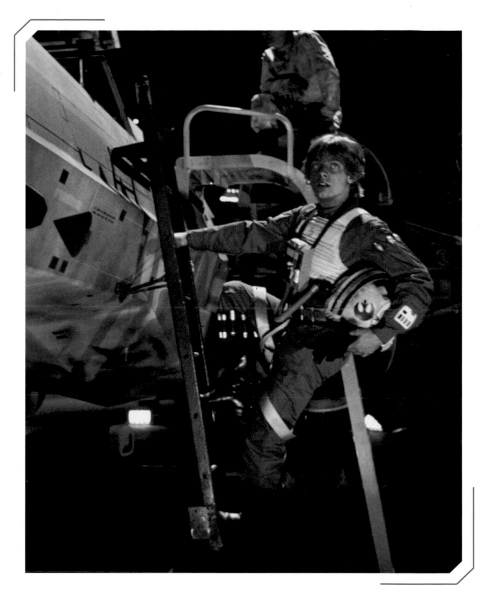

'I'M NOT SUCH A BAD PILOT MYSELF.'

—LUKE SKYWALKER, *STAR WARS*: EPISODE IV *A NEW HOPE*

CHART

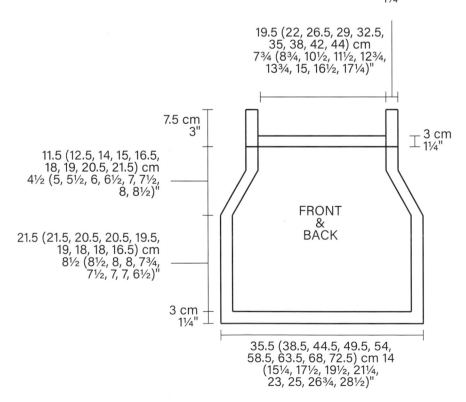

3 cm
1¼"

19.5 (22, 26.5, 29, 32.5,
35, 38, 42, 44) cm
7¾ (8¾, 10½, 11½, 12¾,
13¾, 15, 16½, 17¼)"

7.5 cm
3"

3 cm
1¼"

11.5 (12.5, 14, 15, 16.5,
18, 19, 20.5, 21.5) cm
4½ (5, 5½, 6, 6½, 7, 7½,
8, 8½)"

FRONT
&
BACK

21.5 (21.5, 20.5, 20.5, 19.5,
19, 18, 18, 16.5) cm
8½ (8½, 8, 8, 7¾,
7½, 7, 7, 6½)"

3 cm
1¼"

35.5 (38.5, 44.5, 49.5, 54,
58.5, 63.5, 68, 72.5) cm 14
(15¼, 17½, 19½, 21¼,
23, 25, 26¾, 28½)"

PRINCESS LEIA'S HOTH SNOW GILET

Designed by: **STEPHANIE LOTVEN**

LEVEL: ///

At the beginning of *The Empire Strikes Back*, the rebels are deep in hiding on the ice planet of Hoth. With few signs of life, extremely cold temperatures and a desolate landscape, the rebels outfit themselves in white clothing to remain camouflaged against the snow in the event of an attack. In this classic sequence, Leia wears a quilted white gilet over an insulated jumpsuit. The practical combo keeps her warm until the rebels reach Cloud City.

Worked seamlessly back and forth from the bottom up, this iconic textured gilet is covered with a simple diamond lattice pattern on the bottom half. The top half is worked in stocking stitch, with the shoulders joined using a three-needle cast off. Pick-up-and-knit garter-stitch border bands create an edging on both front openings. Stitches are then picked up and worked in garter stitch, with short row shaping for the collar.

SIZES

XS (S, M, L, XL, 2XL, 3XL, 4XL)
Shown in size S.
Instructions are written for the smallest size, with larger sizes given in brackets; when only one number is given, it applies to all sizes.

FINISHED MEASUREMENTS

Bust: 74.5 (84.5, 94.5, 105, 115, 125, 135.5, 145.5) cm / 29¼ (33¼, 37¼, 41¼, 45¼, 49¼, 53¼, 57¼) in., with 2 cm / ¾ in. overlap

Length: 55 (56.5, 58, 59, 60.5, 61.5, 63, 64) cm / 21¾ (22¼, 22¾, 23¼, 23¾, 24¼, 24¾, 25¼) in.

YARN

Chunky weight (bulky #5) yarn, shown in Cascade Yarns *Ecological Wool* (100% natural Peruvian wool; 437 m / 478 yd per 250 g / 8.82 oz hank), in color #8010 Ecru, 2 (2, 2, 2, 2, 2, 3, 3) hanks

NEEDLES

• 6 mm / US 10, 80 cm / 32 in. long circular needle or size needed to obtain correct tension

NOTIONS

• Stitch markers
• Stitch holders or waste yarn
• Tapestry needle

Continued on page 48

TENSIONS

15 sts and 22 rows = 10 cm / 4 in. in St st

16 sts and 23 rows = 10 cm / 4 in. in Diamond Lattice st

Be sure to check your tensions.

NOTES

- This gilet is worked in one piece from the bottom up. The lower body is worked in a lattice pattern and the yoke is worked in stocking stitch.
- The collar is shaped using short rows. When working past a wrap in garter stitch, it is not necessary to pick up the wrap.

SPECIAL TERMS

LT (left twist): Knit the second stitch on LH needle through the back loop but do not remove st from LH needle, knit the first and second sts tog through the back loops, then slip both sts from LH needle.

RT (right twist): K2tog, but do not remove sts from LH needle, knit first st again, then slip both sts from LH needle.

PATTERN STITCHES

Stocking Stitch (any number of sts)

Knit on RS rows, purl on WS rows.

Garter Stitch (any number of sts)

Knit every row.

Diamond Lattice Stitch (multiple of 8 sts + 2)

Row 1 (RS): K1, *LT, k4, RT; rep from * to last st, k1.

Row 2 & all other WS rows: Purl.

Row 3: K2, *LT, k2, RT, k2; rep from * to end.

Row 5: K3, *LT, RT, k4; rep from * to last 7 sts, LT, RT, k3.

Row 7: K4, *RT, k6; rep from * to last 6 sts, RT, k4.

Row 9: K3, *RT, LT, k4; rep from * to last 3 sts, k3.

Row 11: K2, *RT, k2, LT, k2; rep from * to end.

Row 13: K1, *RT, k4, LT; rep from * to last st, k1.

Row 15: K8, *LT, k6; rep from * to last 2 sts, k2.

Row 16: Purl.

Rep Rows 1–16 for patt.

BODY

CO 114 (130, 146, 162, 178, 194, 210, 226) sts.

Work in Garter st for 2.5 cm / 1 in., ending with a WS row.

Work 2 rows in St st.

Work Rows 1–16 of Diamond Lattice St 4 times, then work Rows 1–15 once more.

Dec row (WS): K1, k2tog, knit to last 3 sts, ssk, k1 – 112 (128, 144, 160, 176, 192, 208, 224) sts rem.

Pm 28 (32, 36, 40, 44, 48, 52, 56) sts from beg and end of row, with 56 (64, 72, 80, 88, 96, 104, 112) sts between markers for back.

DIVIDE FRONTS AND BACK

Next row (RS): *Knit to 2 (2, 3, 3, 3, 4, 4, 4) sts before marker, cast off 4 (4, 6, 6, 6, 8, 8, 8) sts for armhole; rep from * once more, then knit to end of row – 26 (30, 33, 37, 41, 44, 48, 52) sts rem for each front and 52 (60, 66, 74, 82, 88, 96, 104) sts rem for back.

Place sts for right front and back on holders or waste yarn.

LEFT FRONT
SHAPE ARMHOLE

Next row (WS): Purl to last 3 sts, sl 3 wyif.

Dec row (RS): K3, ssk, knit to end of row – 1 st dec'd.

Cont in St st, rep Dec row every RS row 3 (3, 3, 4, 4, 4, 4, 5) more times, then every 4 rows 2 (2, 3, 3, 4, 4, 4, 4) times – 20 (24, 26, 29, 32, 35, 39, 42) sts rem.

Work even until armhole measures 9.5 (9.5, 11, 12, 13.5, 14, 14, 14.5) cm / 3¾ (3¾, 4¼, 4¾, 5¼, 5½, 5½, 5¾) in., ending with a RS row.

SHAPE NECK

Next row (WS): Cast off 3 (3, 3, 4, 4, 4, 4, 5) sts, purl to last 3 sts, sl 3 wyif – 17 (21, 23, 25, 28, 31, 35, 37) sts rem.

Dec row (RS): Knit to last 3 sts, k2tog, k1 – 1 st dec'd.

Dec row (WS): P1, p2tog, purl to last 3 sts, sl 3 wyif – 1 st dec'd.

Dec every row 2 (4, 4, 4, 4, 6, 8, 8) more times, then every RS row 4 (4, 5, 6, 7, 7, 8, 9) times – 9 (11, 12, 13, 15, 16, 17, 18) sts rem.

Cont even until armhole measures approx 17 (18.5, 19.5, 21, 22, 23.5, 25, 26) cm / 6¾ (7¼, 7¾, 8¼, 8¾, 9¼, 9¾, 10¼) in., ending with a WS row. Cut yarn, leaving a tail at least 4 times longer than width of shoulder for joining shoulders. Place sts on holder or waste yarn.

RIGHT FRONT

Place 26 (30, 33, 37, 41, 44, 48, 52) right front sts on needles. Join yarn to beg with a WS row.

SHAPE ARMHOLE

Next row (WS): Purl.

Dec row (RS): Knit to last 5 sts, k2tog, sl 3 wyib – 1 st dec'd.

Cont in St st and rep Dec row every RS row 3 (3, 3, 4, 4, 4, 4, 5) more times, then every 4 rows 2 (2, 3, 3, 4, 4, 4, 4) times – 20 (24, 26, 29, 32, 35, 39, 42) sts rem.

Work even until armhole measures 9.5 (9.5, 11, 12, 13.5, 14, 14, 14.5) cm / 3¾ (3¾, 4¼, 4¾, 5¼, 5½, 5½, 5¾) in., ending with a WS row.

SHAPE NECK

Next row (RS): Cast off 3 (3, 3, 4, 4, 4, 4, 5) sts, knit to last 3 sts, sl 3 wyib – 17 (21, 23, 25, 28, 31, 35, 37) sts rem.

Work 1 row even.

Dec row (RS): K1, ssk, knit to last 3 sts, sl 3 wyib – 1 st dec'd.

Dec row (WS): Purl to last 3 sts, ssp, p1 – 1 st dec'd.

Dec every row 2 (4, 4, 4, 4, 6, 8, 8) more times, then every RS row 4 (4, 5, 6, 7, 7, 8, 9) times – 9 (11, 12, 13, 15, 16, 17, 18) sts rem.

Cont even until armhole measures approx 17 (18.5, 19.5, 21, 22, 23.5, 25, 26) cm / 6¾ (7¼, 7¾, 8¼, 8¾, 9¼, 9¾, 10¼) in., ending with a WS row. Cut yarn, leaving a tail at least 4 times longer than width of shoulder for joining shoulders. Place sts on holder or waste yarn.

BACK

Place 52 (60, 66, 74, 82, 88, 96, 104) back sts on needles. Join yarn to beg with a WS row.

Next row (WS): Purl to last 3 sts, sl 3 wyif.

Dec row (RS): K3, ssk, knit to last 5 sts, k2tog, sl 3 wyib – 2 sts dec'd.

Cont in St st, rep Dec row every RS row 3 (3, 3, 4, 4, 4, 4, 5) more times, then every 4 rows 2 (2, 3, 3, 4, 4, 4, 4) times – 40 (48, 52, 58, 64, 70, 78, 84) sts rem.

Work even until armholes measure 13.5 (14.5, 16, 17, 18.5, 19.5, 21, 21) cm / 5¼ (5¾, 6¼, 6¾, 7¼, 7¾, 8¼, 8¾) in., ending with a WS row.

Pm each side of centre 4 (8, 10, 14, 16, 20, 26, 30) sts for neck.

'I HOPE YOU KNOW WHAT YOU'RE DOING.'

—PRINCESS LEIA, *STAR WARS*: EPISODE V *THE EMPIRE STRIKES BACK*

SHAPE BACK NECK

Next row (RS): Knit to marker, join a second ball of yarn and cast off marked 4 (8, 10, 14, 16, 20, 26, 30) sts, then work to end of row – 18 (20, 21, 22, 24, 25, 26, 27) sts rem for each side.

Work both sides at the same time with separate balls of yarn.

Cast off 3 sts at each neck edge 3 times – 9 (11, 12, 13, 15, 16, 17, 18) sts rem for each side.

Work 1 row even.

FINISHING

Weave in ends. Block lightly.

Join front and back shoulders using Three-Needle Cast Off.

RIGHT FRONT BAND

With RS facing, pick up and knit 2 sts for every 3 rows along right front edge from bottom edge to beg of neck shaping.

Slipping first st of every RS row pwise wyif, work in Garter st for approx 2 cm / ¾ in., ending with a RS row.

Cast off kwise.

LEFT FRONT BAND

With RS facing, pick up and knit 2 sts for every 3 rows along one front edge from beg of neck shaping to bottom edge.

Slipping first st of every WS row pwise wyif, work in Garter st for approx 2 cm / ¾ in., ending with a RS row.

Cast off kwise.

COLLAR

With RS facing, pick up and knit 5 (5, 5, 6, 6, 6, 6, 7) sts along front band and cast-off edge of right front, 3 sts for every 4 rows along shaped edge of right front to shoulder, 22 (26, 28, 32, 34, 38, 44, 48) sts along back neck edge, 3 sts for every 4 rows along shaped edge of left front, then 5 (5, 5, 6, 6, 6, 6, 7) sts along cast-off edge of left front and front band.

Short Row 1 (WS): Sl 1 wyif, knit to last 21 sts, w&t.

Short Row 2 (RS): Knit to last 21 sts, w&t.

Short Row 3: Knit to last w&t, knit wrapped st, then w&t.

Short Row 4: Knit to last w&t, knit wrapped st, then w&t.

Rep last 2 short rows 17 more times.

Next short row (WS): Knit to end.

Next row: Sl 1 wyif, knit to end.

Cast off kwise.

Weave in rem ends.

CHARTS

DIAMOND LATTICE

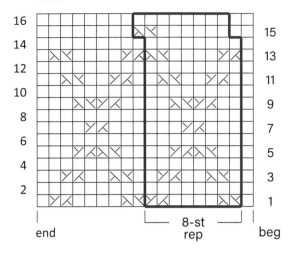

16
14
12
10
8
6
4
2

15
13
11
9
7
5
3
1

end

8-st
rep

beg

KEY

☐ k on RS, p on WS

◺◹ LT

◸◿ RT

☐ pattern repeat

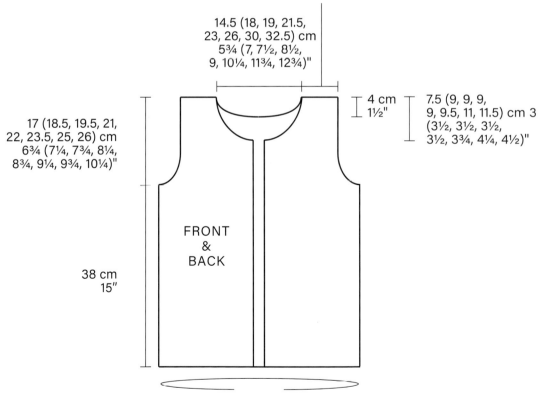

6.5 (7.5, 8.5, 9,
10, 11, 11.5, 12) cm
2½ (3, 3¼, 3½,
4, 4¼, 4½, 4¾)"

14.5 (18, 19, 21.5,
23, 26, 30, 32.5) cm
5¾ (7, 7½, 8½,
9, 10¼, 11¾, 12¾)"

4 cm
1½"

7.5 (9, 9, 9,
9, 9.5, 11, 11.5) cm 3
(3½, 3½, 3½,
3½, 3¾, 4¼, 4½)"

17 (18.5, 19.5, 21,
22, 23.5, 25, 26) cm
6¾ (7¼, 7¾, 8¼,
8¾, 9¼, 9¾, 10¼)"

38 cm
15"

FRONT
&
BACK

72.5 (82.5, 92.5, 103, 113, 123, 133.5, 143.5) cm
28½ (32½, 36½, 40½, 44½, 48½, 52½, 56½)",
not including front bands

REY'S WAISTCOAT AND ARM WRAPS

Designed by: **HEATHER ZOPPETTI**

LEVEL: ////

Episode VII *The Force Awakens* introduces *Star Wars* fans to a new hero: Rey. Thought to have been abandoned by her family as a child, Rey lives on the desert planet Jakku until fate puts her on the path to Luke Skywalker and her ultimate destiny. Rey's costumes in the films are heavily influenced by her upbringing on an arid world and her work as a scavenger. She wears arm warmers to protect her from extreme weather conditions such as sun and sandstorms and she wears long, wispy wraps to aid in climbing as she salvages from ship wreckage. In *The Last Jedi*, Rey still wears arm warmers, but they're made out of a thicker, warmer material, suitable for her destination on an island in the middle of the sea. Her white wraps are replaced with a fitted quilted waistcoat. Together they make a striking costume that adapts perfectly to knitting.

Worked in three separate pieces, the back and two fronts of Rey's waistcoat are worked flat from the bottom up starting at the waist. The shoulders are then joined with a three-needle cast off and the sides are seamed together with mattress stitch. Starting at the waist and worked down, the peplum ends in a feminine picot hem and is then attached to the waist edge. The collar is picked up and knit, then the collar, armhole edges and front openings are finished off with a tidy double crochet edging. Sleeve caps are worked using short rows and then sewn on.

Worked in two parts, the lower piece of the arm wrap is worked flat from the elbow down. Beginning with a picot hem, the arm wrap tapers at the lace wrist, flares out into a stocking-stitch cuff with another picot hem and is then seamed. The upper arm piece is worked as a tapered stocking-stitch band, seamed to form a tube. The elbow piece is worked from the bottom up and sewn onto the lower arm piece.

SIZES

WAISTCOAT

XXS (XS, S, M, L, XL, 2XL, 3XL, 4XL, 5XL)

Shown in size XS.

ARM WRAPS

XS (S, M, L, XL)

Shown in size S.

Instructions are written for the smallest size, with larger sizes given in brackets; when only one number is given, it applies to all sizes.

FINISHED MEASUREMENTS

WAISTCOAT

Bust: 81.5 (92.5, 98, 109, 120.5, 127, 137, 148.5, 160, 166.5) cm / 32 (36½, 38½, 43, 47½, 50, 54, 58½, 63, 65½) in.

Length: 54 (55, 58, 59, 60.5, 61.5, 63, 64, 65.5, 66) cm / 21¼ (21¾, 22¾, 23¼, 23¾, 24¼, 24¾, 25¼, 25¾, 26) in.

LOWER ARM WRAP

Forearm: 21 (24, 26.5, 30, 32.5) cm / 8¼ (9½, 10½, 11¾, 12¾) in.

Length: 30.5 (32, 32.5, 33, 35.5) cm / 12 (12½, 12¾, 13, 14) in.

YARN

DK weight (light #3) yarn, shown in Di Gilpin *Lalland* (100% Scottish lambswool; 175 m / 191 yd per 50 g / 1¾ oz ball), in colour Beechnut

Waistcoat: 5 (5, 6, 7, 7, 8, 9, 9, 10, 11) balls

Arm Wraps: 3 (3, 4, 5, 5) balls

Continued on page 54

NEEDLES

- 3.75 mm / US 5 needles or size needed to obtain correct tension

NOTIONS

- Stitch markers
- Stitch holders or waste yarn
- Tapestry needle
- 3.75 mm / US E-5 crochet hook

TENSIONS

25 sts and 36 rows = 10 cm / 4 in. in Herringbone st

24 sts and 35 rows = 10 cm / 4 in. in St st

Be sure to check your tensions..

NOTES

- The waistcoat is worked in three main pieces. The back and fronts are worked from the bottom up from the waist and joined at the shoulders using Three-Needle Cast Off. The peplum is worked separately from the waist down, ending with a picot hem, and is then sewn to the body at the waist. The collar is picked up from the fronts and back. The front, collar and armhole edges are finished with a row of double crochet. Shoulder pads are worked separately and shaped using short rows, then sewn to the shoulders.

PATTERN STITCHES

Stocking Stitch (any number of sts)

Knit on RS rows, purl on WS rows.

Herringbone Stitch (multiple of 7 + 3 sts)

Row 1 (WS): Sl 1, purl to last st, k1.

Row 2 (RS): Sl 1, *k2tog, k3, LL1, k2; rep from * to last 2 sts, k2.

Row 3: Sl 1, purl to last st, k1.

Row 4: Sl 1, k1, *k3, LL1, k2, k2tog; rep from * to last st, k1.

Rep Rows 1—4 for patt.

SIZES XS (S, M, L, XL, 2XL, 3XL, 4XL, 5XL) ONLY

BO 2 (2, 2, 5, 5, 5, 5, 7, 7) sts at beg of next 2 rows – 87 (94, 98, 100, 107, 115, 124, 130, 135) sts rem.

SIZES M (L, XL, 2XL, 3XL, 4XL, 5XL) ONLY

BO 2 (3, 3, 4, 4, 7, 6) sts at beg of next 2 rows – 94 (94, 101, 107, 116, 116, 123) sts rem.

SIZES 2XL (3XL, 4XL, 5XL) ONLY

BO 3 (4, 4, 4) sts at beg of next 2 rows – 101 (108, 108, 115) sts rem.

ALL SIZES

Cont even until armholes measure 14 (15, 16.5, 18, 18, 19, 19, 20.5, 21.5, 21.5) cm / 5½ (6, 6½, 7, 7, 7½, 7½, 8, 8½, 8½) in.

SHAPE SHOULDERS

Mark centre 26 (29, 36, 36, 36, 41, 41, 44, 46, 51) sts for neck.

Short Rows 1–2: Work to last 4 (4, 4, 4, 4, 5, 5, 5, 5, 5) sts, w&t.

Short Rows 3–4: Work to 4 (4, 4, 4, 4, 5, 5, 5, 5, 5) sts before last turn, w&t.

Short Rows 5–8: Rep Short Rows 3 and 4 twice more.

Next 2 rows: Work in patt to end of row, working all wraps tog with their sts.

Place first 27 (29, 29, 29, 29, 30, 30, 32, 31, 32) sts on holder for shoulder, next 26 (29, 36, 36, 36, 41, 41, 44, 46, 51) sts on holder for neck, then rem 27 (29, 29, 29, 29, 30, 30, 32, 31, 32) sts on holder for shoulder.

LEFT FRONT

CO 38 (45, 52, 59, 66, 66, 73, 80, 87, 94) sts. Knit 1 row.

Beg Herringbone St and working inc sts in St st, inc at beg of RS rows every 12 (12, 12, 10, 12, 12, 12, 12, 12, 10) rows 2 (2, 2, 6, 2, 2, 2, 2, 1, 6) time(s), then every 10 (10, 10, 0, 10, 10, 10, 10, 10, 0) rows 4 (4, 4, 0, 4, 4, 4, 4, 5, 0) times as follows:

Inc Row (RS): Sl 1, M1R, work in established patt to end of row – 1 st inc'd.

WAISTCOAT

BACK

CO 87 (101, 108, 122, 136, 143, 157, 171, 185, 192) sts. Knit 1 row.

Note: Inc rows occur on RS rows. Each RS row of the Herringbone pattern begins with a slipped st and ends with a knit. The inc'd sts should always be worked in St st. You may find it helpful to place markers around the original pattern rep until you are familiar with the st pattern.

Beg Herringbone St and working inc sts in St st, inc every 12 (12, 12, 10, 12, 12, 12, 12, 12, 10) rows 2 (2, 2, 6, 2, 2, 2, 2, 1, 6) time(s), then every 10 (10, 10, 0, 10, 10, 10, 10, 10, 0) rows 4 (4, 4, 0, 4, 4, 4, 4, 5, 0) times as follows:

Inc Row (RS): Sl 1, M1R, work in established patt to last st, M1L, k1 – 2 sts inc'd.

99 (113, 120, 134, 148, 155, 169, 183, 197, 204) sts when inc are complete.

Work even until piece measures approx 20.5 cm / 8 in. from beg, ending with a WS row.

SHAPE ARMHOLES

Cast off 4 (5, 5, 6, 7, 7, 8, 9, 9, 9) sts at beg of next row, then 5 (5, 5, 6, 7, 7, 8, 10, 10, 10) sts at beg of next row – 90 (103, 110, 122, 134, 141, 153, 164, 178, 185) sts rem.

Cast off 3 (4, 4, 6, 6, 6, 7, 8, 9, 9) sts at beg of next 2 rows, then 2 (2, 2, 4, 6, 6, 7, 7, 8, 9) sts at beg of next 2 rows – 80 (91, 98, 102, 110, 117, 125, 134, 144, 149) sts rem.

44 (51, 58, 65, 72, 72, 79, 86, 93, 100) sts
when inc are complete.

Work even until piece measures approx
20.5 cm / 8 in. from beg, ending with
a WS row.

SHAPE ARMHOLE

At beg of RS rows cast off 4 (5, 5, 6, 7, 7, 8,
9, 9, 9) sts once, 3 (4, 4, 6, 6, 6, 7, 8, 9, 9)
sts once, then 2 (2, 2, 4, 6, 6, 7, 7, 8, 9)
sts once – 35 (40, 47, 49, 53, 53, 57, 62,
67, 73) sts rem.

SIZES XS (S, M, L, XL, 2XL, 3XL, 4XL, 5XL) ONLY

At beg of next RS row cast off 2 (2, 2, 5,
5, 5, 5, 7, 7) sts once – 38 (45, 47, 48,
48, 52, 57, 60, 66) sts rem.

SIZES M (L, XL, 2XL, 3XL, 4XL, 5XL) ONLY

At beg of next RS row cast off 2 (3, 3, 4,
4, 7, 6) sts once – 45 (45, 45, 48, 53, 53,
60) sts rem.

SIZES 2XL (3XL, 4XL, 5XL) ONLY

At beg of next RS row cast off 3 (4, 4, 4)
sts once – 45 (49, 49, 56) sts rem.

ALL SIZES

Cont even until armhole measures 14
(15, 16.5, 18, 18, 19, 19, 20.5, 21.5, 21.5)
cm / 5½ (6, 6½, 7, 7, 7½, 7½, 8, 8½,
8½) in., ending with a RS row.

SHAPE SHOULDER

Short Row 1 (WS): Purl to last 4 (4, 4, 4,
4, 5, 5, 5, 5, 5) sts, w&t.

Short Row 2 (RS): Work to end of row.

Short Row 3: Purl to 4 (4, 4, 4, 4, 5, 5, 5,
5, 5) sts before last turn, w&t.

Short Row 4: Work to end of row.

Short Rows 5–8: Rep Short Rows 3 and
4 twice more.

Next row (WS): Purl to end of row,
working all wraps tog with their sts.

With RS facing, place first 27 (29, 29, 29,
29, 30, 30, 32, 31, 32) sts on holder for
shoulder and rem 8 (9, 16, 16, 16, 15,
15, 17, 18, 24) sts on holder for neck.

RIGHT FRONT

CO 38 (45, 52, 59, 66, 66, 73, 80, 87, 94) sts. Knit 1 row.

Beg Herringbone St and working inc sts in St st, inc at end of RS rows every 12 (12, 12, 10, 12, 12, 12, 12, 12, 10) rows 2 (2, 2, 6, 2, 2, 2, 2, 1, 6) time(s), then every 10 (10, 10, 0, 10, 10, 10, 10, 10, 0) rows 4 (4, 4, 0, 4, 4, 4, 4, 5, 0) times as follows:

Inc row (RS): Sl 1, work in established patt to last st, M1L, k1 – 1 st inc'd.

44 (51, 58, 65, 72, 72, 79, 86, 93, 100) sts when inc are complete.

Work even until piece measures approx 20.5 cm / 8 in. from beg, ending with a RS row.

SHAPE ARMHOLE

At beg of WS rows cast off 4 (5, 5, 6, 7, 7, 8, 9, 9, 9) sts once, 3 (4, 4, 6, 6, 6, 7, 8, 9, 9) sts once, then 2 (2, 2, 4, 6, 6, 7, 7, 8, 9) sts once – 35 (40, 47, 49, 53, 53, 57, 62, 67, 73) sts rem.

SIZES XS (S, M, L, XL, 2XL, 3XL, 4XL, 5XL) ONLY

At beg of next WS row cast off 2 (2, 2, 5, 5, 5, 5, 7, 7) sts once – 38 (45, 47, 48, 48, 52, 57, 60, 66) sts rem.

SIZES M (L, XL, 2XL, 3XL, 4XL, 5XL) ONLY

At beg of next WS row cast off 2 (3, 3, 4, 4, 7, 6) sts once – 45 (45, 45, 48, 53, 53, 60) sts rem.

SIZES 2XL (3XL, 4XL, 5XL) ONLY

At beg of next WS row cast off 3 (4, 4, 4) sts once – 45 (49, 49, 56) sts rem.

ALL SIZES

Cont even until armhole measures 14 (15, 16.5, 18, 18, 19, 19, 20.5, 21.5, 21.5) cm / 5½ (6, 6½, 7, 7, 7½ , 7½ , 8, 8½ , 8½) in., ending with a RS row.

SHAPE SHOULDER

Short Row 1 (RS): Work to last 4 (4, 4, 4, 4, 5, 5, 5, 5) sts, w&t.

Short Row 2 (WS): Purl to end of row.

Short Row 3: Work to 4 (4, 4, 4, 4, 5, 5, 5, 5, 5) sts before last turn, w&t.

Short Row 4: Purl to end of row.

Short Rows 5–8: Rep Short Rows 3 and 4 twice more.

Next row (RS): Work to end of row, working all wraps tog with their sts.

Next row (WS): Purl.

With RS facing, place first 8 (9, 16, 16, 16, 15, 15, 17, 18, 24) sts on holder for neck, then 27 (29, 29, 29, 29, 30, 30, 32, 31, 32) sts on holder for shoulder.

PEPLUM

CO 163 (191, 212, 240, 268, 275, 303, 331, 359, 380) sts.

Knit 1 row, inc 22 sts evenly across row – 185 (213, 234, 262, 290, 297, 325, 353, 381, 402) sts.

Work Rows 1–4 of Herringbone St 14 (14, 15, 15, 16, 16, 17, 17, 17, 18) times, ending with a RS row.

PICOT EDGE

Purl 1 row, knit 1 row, purl 1 row.

Fold row (RS): Sl 1, *yo, k2tog; rep from * to last 0 (0, 1, 1, 1, 0, 0, 0, 0, 1) st, k0 (0, 1, 1, 1, 0, 0, 0, 0, 1).

Purl 1 row, knit 1 row.

Cast off all sts loosely pwise.

SHOULDER PADS (MAKE 2)

CO 44 (48, 52, 56, 56, 60, 60, 62, 66, 66) sts.

Row 1 (WS): Sl 1, knit to end of row.

Rep last row twice more. Place marker at centre of row.

SECTION 1

Short Row 1 (RS): Sl 1, knit to 4 (5, 5, 5, 6, 6, 6, 6, 6, 6) sts past centre marker, w&t.

Short Row 2 (WS): Purl to 4 (5, 5, 5, 6, 6, 6, 6, 6, 6) sts past centre marker, w&t.

Short Row 3: Knit to 3 (3, 4, 4, 4, 5, 5, 5, 6, 6) sts past last wrapped st, working wrap tog with its st, w&t.

Short Row 4: Purl to 3 (3, 4, 4, 4, 5, 5, 5, 6, 6) sts past last wrapped st, working wrap tog with its st, w&t.

Short Rows 5–8: Rep Short Rows 3 and 4 twice more.

Short Row 9 (inc): [K3 (3, 3, 3, 3, 4, 4, 4, 5, 5), RLI] 5 times, k2 (4, 10, 10, 12, 8, 8, 8, 4, 4), [LLI, k3 (3, 3, 3, 3, 4, 4, 4, 5, 5)] 5 times, then knit to end of row, working wraps tog with their sts – 54 (58, 62, 66, 66, 70, 70, 72, 76, 76) sts.

Next row (WS): Sl 1, knit to end of row, working wraps tog with their sts.

SECTION 2

Short Row 1 (RS): Sl 1, knit to 5 (5, 5, 6, 6, 6, 7, 7, 7, 7) sts past centre marker, w&t.

Short Row 2 (WS): Purl to 5 (5, 5, 6, 6, 6, 7, 7, 7, 7) sts past centre marker, w&t.

Short Row 3: Knit to 4 (5, 5, 6, 6, 6, 6, 6, 7, 7) sts past last wrapped st, working wrap tog with its st, w&t.

Short Row 4: Purl to 4 (5, 5, 6, 6, 6, 6, 6, 7, 7) sts past last wrapped st, working wrap tog with its st, w&t.

Short Rows 5–8: Rep Short Rows 3 and 4 twice more.

Short Row 9 (inc): [K3 (4, 4, 5, 5, 5, 5, 5, 6, 6), RLI] 5 times, k10 (6, 6, 4, 4, 4, 6, 6, 2, 2), [LLI, k3 (4, 4, 5, 5, 5, 5, 5, 6, 6)] 5 times, then knit to end of row, working wraps tog with their sts – 64 (68, 72, 76, 76, 80, 80, 82, 86, 86) sts.

Next row (WS): Sl 1, knit to end of row, working wraps tog with their sts.

SECTION 3

Short Row 1 (RS): Sl 1, knit to 5 (5, 6, 6, 7, 7, 7, 7, 8, 8) sts past centre marker, w&t.

Short Row 2 (WS): Purl to 5 (5, 6, 6, 7, 7, 7, 7, 8, 8) sts past centre marker, w&t.

Short Row 3: Knit to 6 (7, 7, 7, 7, 8, 8, 8, 8, 8) sts past last wrapped st, working wrap tog with its st, w&t.

Short Row 4: Purl to 6 (7, 7, 7, 7, 8, 8, 8, 8, 8) sts past last wrapped st, working wrap tog with its st, w&t.

Short Rows 5–8: Rep Short Rows 3 and 4 twice more.

Short Row 9 (inc): [K5 (5, 5, 5, 6, 6, 6, 6, 6, 6), RLI] 5 times, k2 (8, 10, 10, 2, 8, 8, 8, 10, 10) slipping the centre marker, [LLI, k5 (5, 5, 5, 6, 6, 6, 6, 6, 6)] 5 times, then knit to end of row, working wraps tog with their sts – 74 (78, 82, 86, 86, 90, 90, 92, 96, 96) sts.

Next row (WS): Sl 1, knit to end of row, working wraps tog with their sts.

SECTION 4

Short Row 1 (RS): Sl 1, knit to 7 (7, 7, 7, 8, 8, 8, 9, 9, 10) sts past centre marker, w&t.

Short Row 2 (WS): Purl to 7 (7, 7, 7, 8, 8, 8, 9, 9, 10) sts past centre marker, w&t.

Short Row 3: Knit to 7 (8, 8, 8, 8, 9, 9, 9, 10, 10) sts past last wrapped st, working wrap tog with its st, w&t.

Short Row 4: Purl to 7 (8, 8, 8, 8, 9, 9, 9, 10, 10) sts past last wrapped st, working wrap tog with its st, w&t.

Short Rows 5–8: Rep Short Rows 3 and 4 twice more.

Short Row 9 (inc): [K6 (6, 6, 6, 6, 7, 7, 7, 8, 8), RLI] 5 times, k2 (8, 8, 4, 10, 6, 6, 8, 4, 10), [LLI, k6 (6, 6, 6, 6, 7, 7, 7, 8, 8)] 5 times, then knit to end of row, working wraps tog with their sts – 84 (88, 92, 96, 96, 100, 100, 102, 106, 106) sts.

Next row (WS): Sl 1, knit to end of row, working wraps tog with their sts.

SECTION 5

Short Row 1 (RS): Sl 1, knit to 9 (9, 9, 9, 9, 10, 10, 10, 11, 11) sts past centre marker, w&t.

Short Row 2 (WS): Purl to 9 (9, 9, 9, 9, 10, 10, 10, 11, 11) sts past centre marker, w&t.

Short Row 3: Knit to 8 (9, 9, 10, 10, 10, 10, 10, 11, 11) sts past last wrapped st, working wrap tog with its st, w&t.

Short Row 4: Purl to 8 (9, 9, 10, 10, 10, 10, 10, 11, 11) sts past last wrapped st, working wrap tog with its st, w&t.

Short Rows 5–8: Rep Short Rows 3 and 4 twice more.

Next row (RS): Knit to end of row, working wrap tog with its st.

Next row (WS): Sl 1, knit to end of row, working wrap tog with its st.

Cast off all sts loosely kwise.

FINISHING

Weave in ends. Lightly block pieces to measurements.

Join fronts and back at shoulders using Three-Needle Cast Off.

Sew side seams.

Seam CO edge of peplum to CO edges of body.

Fold peplum picot edge to inside along fold row and sew to WS.

COLLAR

Note: Collar sts are picked up along the sides of the neck before joining the yarn. In order to pick them up, use the right needle tip to lift the strand at the edge kwise, then on the first row work these sts through the front loop to close any holes.

With RS facing, place 8 (9, 16, 16, 16, 15, 15, 17, 18, 24) held sts for right front neck on needle, pick up 5 (6, 6, 6, 6, 8, 8, 8, 6, 8) sts evenly along side of right front neck, place 26 (29, 36, 36, 36, 41, 41, 44, 46, 51) held sts for back neck on needle, pick up 5 (6, 6, 6, 6, 8, 8, 8, 6, 8) sts evenly along side of left front neck, then place 8 (9, 16, 16, 16, 15, 15, 17, 18, 24) held sts for left front neck – 52 (59, 80, 80, 80, 87, 87, 94, 94, 115) sts.

Join yarn to beg with a WS row. Work in Herringbone St for 12 rows, or until collar measures approx 4 cm / 1½ in., ending with a WS row.

Cast off all sts loosely kwise.

FRONT & COLLAR EDGING

With crochet hook and RS facing, and beg at lower corner of Right Front, work double crochet to top of collar, 3 double crochet in corner, double crochet along top edge of collar, 3 double crochet in corner, then double crochet down left front to bottom corner. Fasten off.

ARMHOLE EDGINGS (MAKE 2)

With crochet hook and RS facing, and beg at centre bottom of armhole, work 1 rnd of double crochet along armhole. Fasten off.

Steam block collar, front, armhole edges and all seams.

Sew shoulder pads to shoulders, lining up centres of shoulder pads with shoulder seams, and top st along shoulder pad cast-off edge and side edges, leaving armhole edge free to hang over as a cap.

Weave in rem ends.

ARM WRAPS
LOWER ARM (MAKE 2)

CO 52 (59, 66, 73, 80) sts.

Row 1 (WS): Sl 1, purl to last st, k1.

Row 2 (RS): Sl 1, knit to end of row.

Rep Row 1.

Fold row (RS): Sl 1, *yo, k2tog; rep from * to last 1 (0, 1, 0, 1) st, k1 (0, 1, 0, 1).

Rep Rows 1 and 2 once more.

Beg Herringbone St and dec every 6 rows 4 (6, 6, 7, 9) times, then every 4 rows 7 (5, 5, 4, 2) times, ending with a RS row, as follows:

Dec row (RS): Sl 1, ssk, work in established patt to last 3 sts, k2tog, k1 – 2 sts dec'd.

30 (37, 44, 51, 58) sts rem when dec are complete.

LACE CUFF

Work Rows 1–21 of Lace Chart.

FLARED CUFF

Inc row (RS): Sl 1, k2, M1R, knit to last 3 sts, M1L, k3 – 2 sts inc'd.

Next row (WS): Sl 1, k2, purl to last 3 sts, k3.

Rep last 2 rows 12 (12, 14, 14, 16) more times – 56 (63, 74, 81, 92) sts.

PICOT EDGE

Row 1 (RS): Sl 1, knit to end of row.

Row 2 (WS): Sl 1, purl to last st, k1.

Fold row (RS): Sl 1, *yo, k2tog; rep from * to last 1 (0, 1, 0, 1) st, k1 (0, 1, 0, 1).

Rep Row 2 once, then rep Row 1 again.

Cast off all sts loosely pwise.

ARM PADS (MAKE 2)

CO 17 (20, 23, 26, 29) sts.

Work in St st for 13 (14, 14, 14, 15) rows, ending with a WS row.

Row 1 (RS): Sl 1, purl to last st, k1.

Row 2 (WS): Sl 1, knit to last st.

Work in St st for 10 (12, 12, 14, 14) rows.

Rep last 12 (14, 14, 16, 16) rows 3 more times, then work Rows 1 and 2 again. *AT THE SAME TIME*, inc at each end of every 14 (16, 16, 16, 16) rows 4 (2, 2, 3, 4) times, then every 12 (14, 14, 14, 14) rows 1 (3, 3, 2, 1) time(s), ending with a WS row, as follows:

Inc row (RS): Sl 1, M1R, work in established patt to last st, M1L, k1 –2 sts inc'd.

27 (30, 33, 36, 39) sts when inc are complete.

ELBOW PAD

Cast off 5 sts at beg of next 2 rows – 17 (20, 23, 26, 29) sts rem.

Row 1 (RS): Sl 1, knit to end of row.

Row 2 (WS): Sl 1, purl to last st, k1.

Rep last 2 rows twice more.

Dec row (RS): Sl 1, ssk, knit to last 3 sts, k2tog, k1 – 2 sts dec'd.

Next row (WS): Sl 1, purl to last st, k1.

Rep last 2 rows twice more – 11 (14, 17, 20, 23) sts rem.

Inc row (RS): Sl 1, M1R, knit to last st, M1L, k1 – 2 sts inc'd.

Next row (WS): Sl 1, purl to last st, k1.

Rep last 2 rows twice more – 17 (20, 23, 26, 29) sts.

Work 6 rows even.

Cast off all sts loosely pwise.

RIGHT UPPER ARM WRAP

CO 1 st.

Row 1 (RS, inc): K1f&b – 2 sts.

Row 2 (WS): Purl.

Row 3 (inc): K1, M1R, k1 – 3 sts.

Row 4: Sl 1, p1, k1.

Row 5 (inc): Sl 1, M1R, knit to end – 1 st inc'd.

Row 6: Sl 1, purl to last st, k1.

Rep last 2 rows 8 times – 12 sts.

Work even in St st until piece measures approx 106 (146, 187.5, 235, 270.5) cm / 41¾ (57½, 73¾, 92½, 106½) in. from last inc, ending with a WS row.

Dec row (RS): Sl 1, knit to last 3 sts, k2tog, k1 –1 st dec'd.

Next row (WS): Sl 1, purl to last st, k1.

Rep last 2 rows 8 more times – 3 sts rem.

Dec row (RS): K1, k2tog – 2 sts rem.

Next row (WS): Purl.

Dec row: K2tog – 1 st rem. Fasten off.

LEFT UPPER ARM WRAP

CO 1 st.

Row 1 (RS, inc): K1f&b – 2 sts.

Row 2 (WS): Purl.

Row 3 (inc): K1, M1L, k1 – 3 sts.

Row 4: Sl 1, p1, k1.

Row 5 (inc): Sl 1, knit to last st, M1L, k1 – 1 st inc'd.

Row 6: Sl 1, purl to last st, k1.

Rep last 2 rows 8 times – 12 sts.

Work even in St st until piece measures approx 106 (146, 187.5, 235, 270.5) cm / 41¾ (57½, 73¾, 92½, 106½) in. from last inc, ending with a WS row.

Dec row (RS): Sl 1, ssk, knit to end of row – 1 st dec'd.

Next row (WS): Sl 1, purl to last st, k1.

Rep last 2 rows 8 more times – 3 sts rem.

Dec row (RS): K1, ssk – 2 sts rem.

Next row (WS): Purl.

Dec row: Ssk – 1 st rem. Fasten off.

FINISHING

Weave in ends. Lightly block pieces to measurements.

Fold top of elbow pads to inside, matching inc and dec sections to make a double thickness of fabric at the top of the arm pads, then sew to WS.

Sew arm pads to lower arm pieces, making sure they are on opposite sides; the arm pads should be on the top of the arm when worn.

Fold picot hems to inside along fold rows, and sew cast-off edge to WS.

Sew side edges of lower arm pieces to beg of flared cuff; leave flared section open.

Winding strip for upper arm wraps around your arm for best fit, taper the wrap so that it starts at the upper arm and ends at the elbow. Carefully remove the wrap from your arm and sew the edges of the strip tog using a modified mattress st: insert tapestry needle into upper wrap as usual, then backwards into the lower piece so that the st appears on the front of the work.

Weave in rem ends.

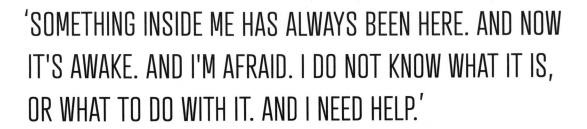

'SOMETHING INSIDE ME HAS ALWAYS BEEN HERE. AND NOW IT'S AWAKE. AND I'M AFRAID. I DO NOT KNOW WHAT IT IS, OR WHAT TO DO WITH IT. AND I NEED HELP.'

—REY, *STAR WARS*: EPISODE VIII *THE LAST JEDI*

CHARTS

HERRINGBONE ST

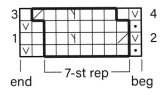

LACE CHART

KEY

☐ k on RS, p on WS

⊡ p on RS, k on WS

⊙ yo

◹ k2tog

◺ ssk

▽ sl 1 wyib on RS, sl 1 wyif on WS

⅄ LLI

◼ repeat

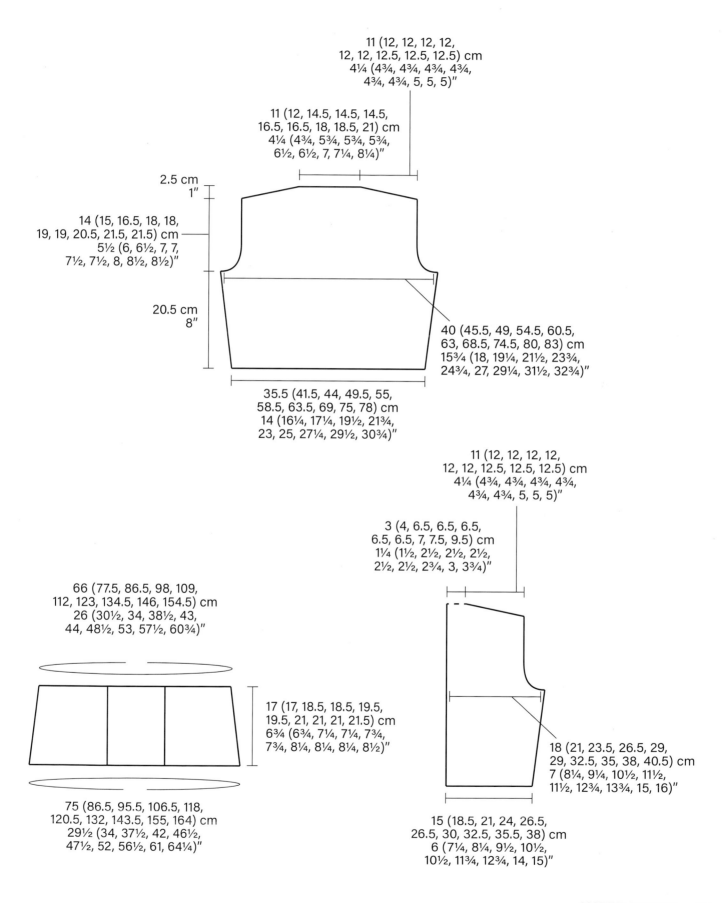

11 (12, 12, 12, 12,
12, 12, 12.5, 12.5, 12.5) cm
4¼ (4¾, 4¾, 4¾, 4¾,
4¾, 4¾, 5, 5, 5)"

11 (12, 14.5, 14.5, 14.5,
16.5, 16.5, 18, 18.5, 21) cm
4¼ (4¾, 5¾, 5¾, 5¾,
6½, 6½, 7, 7¼, 8¼)"

2.5 cm
1"

14 (15, 16.5, 18, 18,
19, 19, 20.5, 21.5, 21.5) cm
5½ (6, 6½, 7, 7,
7½, 7½, 8, 8½, 8½)"

20.5 cm
8"

40 (45.5, 49, 54.5, 60.5,
63, 68.5, 74.5, 80, 83) cm
15¾ (18, 19¼, 21½, 23¾,
24¾, 27, 29¼, 31½, 32¾)"

35.5 (41.5, 44, 49.5, 55,
58.5, 63.5, 69, 75, 78) cm
14 (16¼, 17¼, 19½, 21¾,
23, 25, 27¼, 29½, 30¾)"

11 (12, 12, 12, 12,
12, 12, 12.5, 12.5, 12.5) cm
4¼ (4¾, 4¾, 4¾, 4¾,
4¾, 4¾, 5, 5, 5)"

3 (4, 6.5, 6.5, 6.5,
6.5, 6.5, 7, 7.5, 9.5) cm
1¼ (1½, 2½, 2½, 2½,
2½, 2½, 2¾, 3, 3¾)"

66 (77.5, 86.5, 98, 109,
112, 123, 134.5, 146, 154.5) cm
26 (30½, 34, 38½, 43,
44, 48½, 53, 57½, 60¾)"

17 (17, 18.5, 18.5, 19.5,
19.5, 21, 21, 21, 21.5) cm
6¾ (6¾, 7¼, 7¼, 7¾,
7¾, 8¼, 8¼, 8¼, 8½)"

18 (21, 23.5, 26.5, 29,
29, 32.5, 35, 38, 40.5) cm
7 (8¼, 9¼, 10½, 11½,
11½, 12¾, 13¾, 15, 16)"

75 (86.5, 95.5, 106.5, 118,
120.5, 132, 143.5, 155, 164) cm
29½ (34, 37½, 42, 46½,
47½, 52, 56½, 61, 64¼)"

15 (18.5, 21, 24, 26.5,
26.5, 30, 32.5, 35.5, 38) cm
6 (7¼, 8¼, 9½, 10½,
10½, 11¾, 12¾, 14, 15)"

PADMÉ'S BATTLE WRAP

Designed by: **TRYSTEN MOLINA**

LEVEL: ✎

In *Attack of the Clones*, Padmé Amidala, former Queen and current Senator of Naboo in the Galactic Republic Congress, joins Anakin Skywalker in battle to attempt to rescue Obi-Wan Kenobi from Count Dooku. Strong willed, regal and quick thinking, Padmé can hold her own in a fight and is essential in ensuring their survival in the arena on Geonosis. While most of Padmé's costumes are made out of flowing silk and lace, the wrap she wears in the conveyor belt scene on Geonosis is thick and warm – the perfect garment for a *Star Wars* fan looking for a simple costume replica project.

Knit in two pieces, the first piece is worked from the outside in, starting with a twisted rib edging. An easy knit-and-purl basketweave pattern is then worked to the middle, and the centre stitches are put on hold. After the back piece is worked, the long edges are joined using a three-needle cast off, with the centre stitches joined into the round and worked in a twisted rib collar. Wear your battle wrap long and open, or wrap it around your shoulders and secure it with your favourite shawl pin.

SIZE
One size

FINISHED MEASUREMENTS
Width: 195.5 cm / 77 in., edge to edge
Front Length: 28.5 cm / 11¼ in.
Back Length: 42.5 cm / 16¾ in.

YARN
Aran weight (medium #4) yarn, shown in Dragon Hoard Yarn *Storyteller Worsted* (100% superwash merino wool; 198 m / 217 yd per 100 g / 3½ oz hank), in colour Feather, 9 hanks

NEEDLES
• 4 mm / US 6, 40 cm / 16 in. cm long circular needle
• 5 mm / US 8, 150 cm / 60 in. long circular needle or size needed to obtain correct tension

NOTIONS
• Stitch marker
• Waste yarn
• Spare 5 mm / US 8, 80 cm / 32 in. long circular needle
• Tapestry needle

TENSION
16 sts and 30 rows = 10 cm / 4 in. in Basketweave with larger needles
Be sure to check your tension.

Continued on page 66

PATTERN STITCHES

Garter Stitch (any number of sts)

Knit every row.

K1, P1 Rib (even number of sts)

Row 1 (RS): *K1, p1; rep from * to end of row.

Row 2 (WS): *K1, p1; rep from * to end of row.

Rep Rows 1 and 2 for patt.

Basketweave Pattern (multiple of 6 sts + 2)

Row 1 (RS): Sl 1 wyib, knit to end of row.

Row 2 (WS): Sl 1 wyib, k3, purl to last 4 sts, k4.

Row 3: Sl 1 wyib, k3, *k2, p4; rep from * to last 4 sts, k4.

Row 4: Sl 1 wyib, k3, *k4, p2; rep from * to last 4 sts, k4.

Rows 5 and 6: Rep Rows 3 and 4.

Rows 7 and 8: Rep Rows 1 and 2.

Row 9: Sl 1 wyib, k3, p3, *k2, p4; rep from * to last 7 sts, k2, p1, k4.

Row 10: Sl 1 wyib, *k4, p2; rep from * to last 7 sts, k7.

Rows 11 and 12: Rep Rows 9 and 10.

Rep Rows 1–12 of patt.

NOTES

- The front and back of this shawl are worked separately, then joined at the shoulders using Three-Needle Cast Off.
- The shorter section is the front.

FRONT

With smaller cir needle, CO 308 sts using Twisted German method.

Row 1 (RS): Sl 1 wyib, k3, work in K1, P1 Rib to last 4 sts, k4.

Row 2 (WS): Sl 1 wyib, k3, work in established ribbing to last 4 sts, k4.

Rep last 2 rows once more.

Change to larger cir needle.

Work Rows 1–12 of Basketweave patt 6 times, then work Rows 1–7 once more. Piece should measure approx 28.5 cm / 11¼ in. from beg.

Place first 134 sts on one piece of waste yarn for shoulder, next 40 sts on second piece of waste yarn for neck, then rem 134 sts on third piece of waste yarn for shoulder.

BACK

With smaller cir needle, CO 308 sts using Twisted German method.

Row 1 (RS): Sl 1 wyib, k3, work in K1, P1 Rib to last 4 sts, k4.

Row 2 (WS): Sl 1 wyib, k3, work in established ribbing to last 4 sts, k4.

Rep last 2 rows once more.

Change to larger cir needle.

Work Rows 1–12 of Basketweave patt 10 times. Piece should measure approx 42.5 cm / 16¾ in. from beg.

FINISHING

Place 134 sts of right front on spare cir needle. Holding both pieces with RS tog (WS facing out), join shoulder using Three-Needle Cast Off. Fasten off rem st on RH needle.

Rep with rem shoulder sts.

NECKBAND

Place rem 40 front sts on spare cir needle.

With smaller cir needle and RS facing, pick up and knit 1 st in front of gap between front and back sts, k40 front sts from spare cir needle, pick up and knit 2 sts in gap between front and back sts, k40 back sts from larger cir needle, then pick up and knit 1 st in back half of gap between front and back sts – 84 sts. Pm and join to work in the rnd.

Rnd 1: *K1, p1; rep from * to end of rnd.

Rep last rnd 8 more times.

Cast off all sts loosely in patt.

Weave in ends. Block to measurements.

BEHIND THE SCENES:

One of the most iconic wardrobes in the entire series, Queen Amidala's early costumes and make-up are heavily influenced by the Japanese kimono and the clothing of Mongolian royalty. Costume designer Trisha Biggar gathered a blend of modern and antique textiles and trimmings to get the perfect look, and many of the costumes took months to complete. As the films progress and we see more of Padmé's personal life, her costumes shift to more flowing fabrics and softer colours.

ANAKIN SKYWALKER: 'YOU CALL THIS A DIPLOMATIC SOLUTION?'
PADMÉ AMIDALA: 'NO, I CALL IT AGGRESSIVE NEGOTIATIONS.'

—STAR WARS: EPISODE II *ATTACK OF THE CLONES*

CHARTS

BASKETWEAVE CHART

KEY

☐ k on RS, p on WS

▫ p on RS, k on WS

☑ sl 1 wyib on RS

☒ sl 1 wyib on WS

▣ pattern repeat

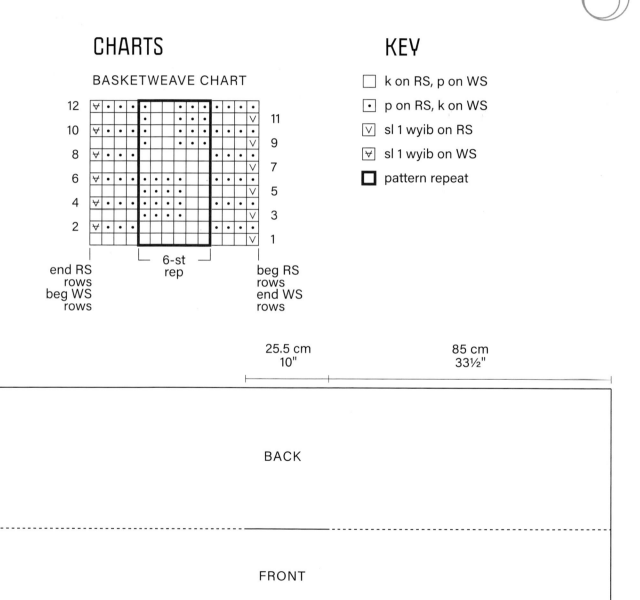

INSPIRED
APPAREL

'DO. OR DO NOT. THERE IS NO TRY.'

–YODA, *STAR WARS*: EPISODE V *THE EMPIRE STRIKES BACK*

THE ORDER OF THE JEDI PULLOVER

Designed by: **MEGHAN REGAN**

LEVEL: ////

Acultural juggernaut, *Star Wars* has enchanted audiences for over forty years with its classic tale of good versus evil. When *A New Hope* burst onto the scene in 1977, science fiction was largely considered to be the domain of niche fans and comic collectors. But audiences from all backgrounds found someone to relate to in *Star Wars* – a farm boy with big dreams, a forward-thinking princess, a ne'er-do-well smuggler – and pretty soon Luke, Leia and Han became household names, along with terms like *lightsaber*, *the Force*, and *Jedi*. Shattering box office records for decades and pushing the envelope in technology, the series has now expanded to include spin-off films, novels, games and multiple critically acclaimed TV series, making *Star Wars* one of the biggest – and most beloved – pop culture franchises today.

Featuring key elements related to the Jedi order like lightsabers, exploding stars, Master Yoda and the Jedi Order symbol in stranded colourwork, this top-down garment starts with the yoke before splitting for the sleeves. The colourwork pattern continues past the armholes, then the body is worked in stocking stitch. The held sleeve stitches are then picked up and worked in stocking stitch. Block and wear proudly!

SIZES

XS (S, M, L, XL, 2XL, 3XL, 4XL, 5XL, 6XL)

Shown in size S.

Instructions are written for the smallest size, with larger sizes given in brackets; when only one number is given, it applies to all sizes.

FINISHED MEASUREMENTS

Bust: 87 (96.5, 106.5, 116, 125.5, 135.5, 145.5, 155, 164.5, 174) cm / 34¼ (38, 42, 45¾, 49½, 53¼, 57¼, 61, 64¾, 68½) in.

Length from centre back: 65 (66, 67.5, 68.5, 70, 71, 72.5, 73.5, 75, 76) cm / 25½ (26, 26½, 27, 27½, 28, 28½, 29, 29½, 30) in.

YARN

Aran weight (medium #4), shown in Hazel Knits *Cadence* (100% superwash merino wool; (183 m / 200 yd per 110 g /3.88 oz hank)

Main Colour (MC): Signature Black, 5 (5, 6, 6, 6, 7, 7, 8, 8, 9) hanks

Contrast Colour 1 (CC1): City Lights, 1 hank

Contrast Colour 2 (CC2): Fresh Cut, 1 hank

Contrast Colour 3 (CC3): Superhero, 1 hank

Contrast Colour 4 (CC4): Mirror, 1 (1, 1, 1, 1, 2, 2, 2, 2, 2) hank(s)

Continued on page 74

PULLOVER

YOKE

With shorter smaller cir needle and MC, CO 72 (82, 86, 92, 94, 94, 94, 94, 94) sts. Pm and join to work in the rnd, being careful not to twist sts. Rnds beg at centre of back.

Work in K1, P1 Rib for 8 rnds.

Change to shorter larger cir needle.

Knit 1 rnd.

Inc rnd: Knit and inc 0 (0, 0, 0, 4, 12, 16, 20, 26, 32) sts evenly spaced – 72 (82, 86, 92, 98, 106, 110, 114, 120, 126) sts.

SHAPE BACK NECK

Short Row 1 (RS): K25 (26, 28, 29, 29, 29, 29, 29, 29) sts, w&t.

Short Row 2 (WS): P25 (26, 28, 29, 29, 29, 29, 29, 29) sts, sm, p25 (26, 28, 29, 29, 29, 29, 29, 29).

Short Row 3: Knit to 2 sts before last wrap, w&t.

Short Row 4: Purl to 2 sts before the last wrap, w&t.

Short Rows 5–10: Rep last 2 short rows 3 more times.

Short Row 11: Knit to beg-of-rnd marker.

Inc rnd 1: *K2, M1; rep from * to end of rnd, working wraps tog with their sts as you come to them – 108 (123, 129, 138, 147, 159, 165, 171, 180, 189) sts.

Next rnd: Knit and inc 4 (5, 7, 6, 13, 17, 19, 21, 28, 27) sts evenly spaced – 112 (128, 136, 144, 160, 176, 184, 192, 208, 216) sts.

Work Rnds 1–7 of Chart A.

Work 0 (1, 1, 1, 1, 1, 2, 2, 2, 2) rnd(s) even with MC only.

Inc Rnd 2: *K2, M1; rep from * to end of rnd – 168 (192, 204, 216, 240, 264, 276, 288, 312, 324) sts.

Work 0 (0, 0, 1, 2, 2, 2, 2, 2, 2) rnd(s) even with MC only.

Work Rnds 1–8 of Chart B.

Work 0 (1, 1, 1, 1, 2, 2, 2, 2, 3) rnd(s) even with MC only.

Inc Rnd 3: *K3, M1; rep from * to end of rnd – 224 (256, 272, 288, 320, 352, 368, 384, 416, 432) sts.

Work 0 (0, 1, 1, 2, 2, 3, 3, 3) rnd(s) even with MC only.

Work Rnds 1–17 of Chart C.

Work 0 (1, 1, 1, 2, 2, 3, 3, 4, 4) rnd(s) even with MC only.

Inc Rnd 4: *K4, M1; rep from * to end of rnd – 280 (320, 340, 360, 400, 440, 460, 480, 520, 540) sts.

Work 0 (0, 1, 1, 2, 3, 3, 4, 4, 5) rnd(s) even with MC only.

Work Rnds 1–16 of Chart D.

Work 0 (1, 1, 2, 2, 3, 3, 4, 5, 6) rnd(s) even with MC only.

Inc Rnd 5: Knit and inc 4 sts evenly spaced – 284 (324, 344, 364, 404, 444, 464, 484, 524, 544) sts.

Work 0 (0, 1, 2, 2, 3, 3, 4, 6, 6) rnd(s) even with MC only.

Piece should measure approx 23 (24, 25.5, 26.5, 28, 29, 30.5, 32, 33, 34.5) cm / 9 (9½, 10, 10½, 11, 11½, 12, 12½, 13, 13½) in. from CO at centre of front.

DIVIDE BODY AND SLEEVES

Next rnd: With MC only, k42 (49, 52, 56, 63, 70, 74, 77, 85, 88) sts for right back, place next 58 (64, 68, 70, 76, 82, 84, 88, 92, 96) sts on holder or waste yarn for right sleeve, CO 6 (2, 6, 8, 4, 0, 2, 6, 0, 4) sts using Backward Loop method and pm for new beg of rnd at centre of these CO sts, k84 (98, 104, 112, 126, 140, 148, 154, 170, 176) sts for front, place next 58 (64, 68, 70, 76, 82, 84, 88, 92, 96) on holder or waste yarn for left sleeve, CO 6 (2, 6, 8, 4, 0, 2, 6, 0, 4) sts and pm at centre of these CO sts, k42 (49, 52, 56, 63, 70, 74, 77, 85, 88) sts for left back, remove old beg-of-rnd marker, knit to new beg-of-rnd marker – 180 (200, 220, 240, 260, 280, 300, 320, 340, 360) sts.

BODY

Work Rnds 1–43 of Chart E.

For a straighter body below Chart E, dec 8 (10, 10, 12, 12, 14, 14, 14, 16, 18) sts evenly spaced across first rnd after chart – 172 (190, 210, 228, 248, 266, 286, 306, 324, 342) sts will rem. When dividing for the hem, work half the number of sts for each half of the hem.

Cont even in St st with MC only until body measures 33 cm / 13 in. from underarm CO.

DIVIDE HEM

Change to longer smaller cir needle.

Row 1 (RS): *K1, p1; rep from * to marker, turn and leave rem 90 (100, 110, 120, 130, 140, 150, 160, 170, 180) sts unworked on larger cir needle – 90 (100, 110, 120, 130, 140, 150, 160, 170, 180) sts rem.

Row 2 (WS): Sl 1 wyif, *p1, k1; rep from * to last st, p1.

Row 3: Sl 1 wyif, *p1, k1; rep from * to last st, p1.

Rep last 2 rows until ribbing measures 5 cm / 2 in.

Cast off loosely in ribbing.

Work rem half of hem same as first.

SLEEVES

Place 58 (64, 68, 70, 76, 82, 84, 88, 92, 96) sleeve sts on larger dpn.

With MC, beg at centre of underarm CO, pick up and knit 3 (1, 3, 4, 2, 0, 1, 3, 1, 2) st(s), knit sleeve sts, then pick up and knit 3 (1, 3, 4, 2, 0, 1, 3, 1, 2) st(s) along rem underarm CO. Pm and join to work in the rnd – 64 (66, 74, 78, 80, 82, 86, 94, 94, 100) sts. *For size 5XL, because no sts have been cast on at bottom of armhole, pick up the sts on each side of gap between front and back.*

Working in St st, work 2 rnds even.

Dec rnd: K1, k2tog, knit to last 3 sts, ssk, 1 – 2 sts dec'd.

Rep Dec rnd every other rnd 10 (11, 14, 16, 16, 17, 18, 21, 21, 23) more times – 42 (42, 44, 44, 46, 46, 48, 50, 50, 52) sts rem.

Cont even until sleeve measures approx 37 (37, 37, 38, 38, 38.5, 38.5, 38, 37.5, 37.5) cm / 14½ (14½, 14½, 15, 15, 15¼, 15¼, 15, 14¾, 14¾) in. from underarm.

Change to smaller dpn.

Work in K1, P1 Rib for 5 cm / 2 in.

Cast off loosely in ribbing.

FINISHING

Weave in ends. Block to measurements.

CHARTS

A
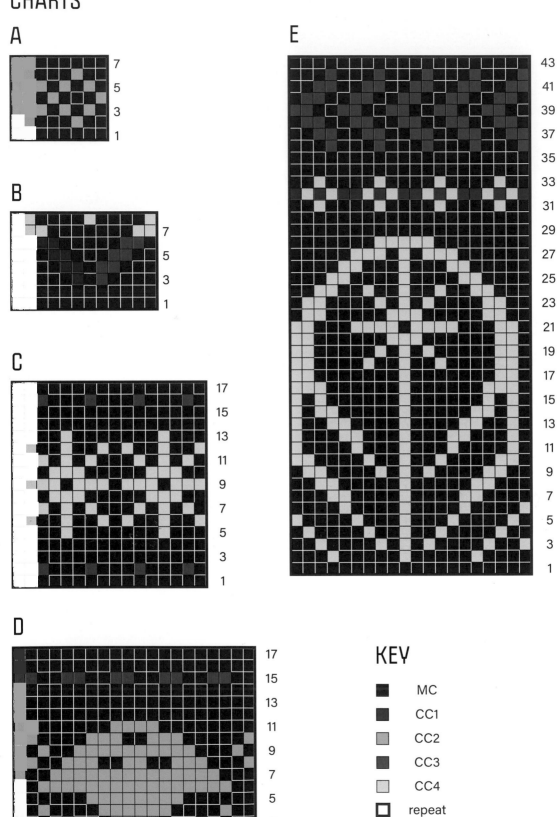

7
5
3
1

B

7
5
3
1

C

17
15
13
11
9
7
5
3
1

D

17
15
13
11
9
7
5
3
1

E

43
41
39
37
35
33
31
29
27
25
23
21
19
17
15
13
11
9
7
5
3
1

KEY

■ MC
■ CC1
■ CC2
■ CC3
■ CC4
□ repeat

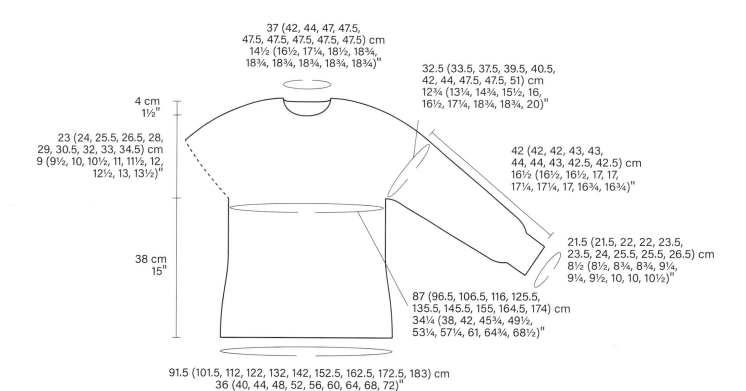

37 (42, 44, 47, 47.5,
47.5, 47.5, 47.5, 47.5, 47.5) cm
14½ (16½, 17¼, 18½, 18¾,
18¾, 18¾, 18¾, 18¾, 18¾)"

32.5 (33.5, 37.5, 39.5, 40.5,
42, 44, 47.5, 47.5, 51) cm
12¾ (13¼, 14¾, 15½, 16,
16½, 17¼, 18¾, 18¾, 20)"

4 cm
1½"

23 (24, 25.5, 26.5, 28,
29, 30.5, 32, 33, 34.5) cm
9 (9½, 10, 10½, 11, 11½, 12,
12½, 13, 13½)"

42 (42, 42, 43, 43,
44, 44, 43, 42.5, 42.5) cm
16½ (16½, 16½, 17, 17,
17¼, 17¼, 17, 16¾, 16¾)"

38 cm
15"

21.5 (21.5, 22, 22, 23.5,
23.5, 24, 25.5, 25.5, 26.5) cm
8½ (8½, 8¾, 8¾, 9¼,
9¼, 9½, 10, 10, 10½)"

87 (96.5, 106.5, 116, 125.5,
135.5, 145.5, 155, 164.5, 174) cm
34¼ (38, 42, 45¾, 49½,
53¼, 57¼, 61, 64¾, 68½)"

91.5 (101.5, 112, 122, 132, 142, 152.5, 162.5, 172.5, 183) cm
36 (40, 44, 48, 52, 56, 60, 64, 68, 72)"

EWOK HOOD

Designed by: **CARISSA BROWNING**

LEVEL: ╱

Living on the forest moon of Endor, Ewoks are a forest-dwelling species who build their homes high in the trees. Short, furry aliens with big ears and bright eyes, they befriend the rebels as they attempt to bring down the shield generator for the second Death Star. Providing key information and much-needed battle assistance, these hood-wearing tribe members carry primitive weapons, which prove to be imperative in defeating the technology-dependent Empire.

Beginning at the lower edge, the hood is worked from the bottom up in the round in garter stitch. German short row shaping is used to create three wedges that curve the hood upwards and over the back of the head. Faux fur pom-poms are attached for Ewok ears. With sizing from toddler through adult, you can make one for every member of your tribe!

SIZES

XS (S, M, L, XL)

To fit: Toddler (Child, Teen, Adult Small, Adult Large)

Shown in size S.

Instructions are written for the smallest size, with larger sizes given in brackets; when only one number is given, it applies to all sizes.

FINISHED MEASUREMENTS

Circumference: 56 (61, 66, 71, 76) cm / 22 (24, 26, 28, 30) in.

Front Height: 10 (11.5, 12.5, 14, 15) cm / 4 (4½, 5, 5½, 6) in., to bottom of opening

Back Height: 44 (47, 52, 55, 60.5) cm / 17½ (18½, 20½, 21¾, 23¾) in. along curve at centre back

YARN

Aran weight (medium #4) yarn, shown in Quince and Co *Owl Tweet* (50% American wool, 50% alpaca; 110 m / 120 yd per 50 g / 1¾ oz hank) in colour Russet, 2 (3, 3, 3, 4) hanks

NEEDLES

- 4.5 mm / US 7, 40 cm / 16 in. or 60 cm / 24 in. long circular needle or size needed to obtain correct tension

NOTIONS

- Stitch markers
- Tapestry needle
- Two faux fur pom-poms, approx 10 cm / 4 in. diameter
- Two snaps (optional)
- Two buttons and elastic (optional)

Continued on page 82

HOOD

NECK

CO 88 (96, 104, 112, 120) sts. Pm and join to work in the rnd, being careful not to twist sts.

Purl 1 rnd.

Knit 1 rnd.

Cont in garter st until there are 14 (16, 18, 20, 22) garter ridges on RS, ending with a purl rnd.

SHAPE HOOD

Short Row 1 (RS): K55 (61, 65, 71, 75), turn.

Short Row 2 (WS): Pm for short row, sl 1 pwise wyif, pull yarn tightly up and over RH needle to create a double st (DS), k21 (25, 25, 29, 29), turn.

Short Row 3: Pm for short row, DS, knit to 1 st before marker, knit both legs of DS tog, remove marker, k2, turn.

Rep last short row until 1 st rem unworked on each side between final DS and beg-of-rnd marker. End with a WS short row.

Last short row (RS): Pm for short row, DS, knit to 1 st before next marker, knit both legs of DS tog, remove marker, k1. Do not turn.

Next rnd: P1, remove marker, purl both legs of DS tog, purl to end of rnd.

Rep from Short Row 1 two more times.

FACE EDGE

Knit 1 rnd.

Purl 1 rnd.

Cast off all sts loosely kwise.

FINISHING

Weave in ends. Block to finished measurements.

Attach each pom-pom approx 5 (5, 5.5, 5.5, 6.5) cm / 2 (2, 2¼, 2¼, 2½) in. on either side of centre top of hood, and 10 (10, 11.5, 11.5, 12.5) cm / 4 (4, 4½, 4½, 5) in. from face edge by sewing snaps to hood and pom-poms. Alternatively, sew buttons to WS of hood, thread elastic from RS to WS, then back to RS at each button, loop elastic around button, then pull elastic tight to snug pom-pom to hood and securely attach elastic to each pom-pom.

'YOU'RE A JITTERY LITTLE THING, AREN'T YOU?'

—PRINCESS LEIA, *STAR WARS*: EPISODE VI *RETURN OF THE JEDI*

STARFIGHTER SCARF

Designed by: **JESSICA GODDARD**

LEVEL: ////

Starfighters are imperative for space travel, but their design inspiration comes from planet Earth. *Star Wars* creator George Lucas had model makers look to World War II aircrafts such as TBF torpedo bombers for the Y-wing and small crafts used in aerial dogfighting for the X-wing. Different-coloured lasers are a visual shorthand to determine which side the starfighters belong to – the Empire's TIE fighters fire green lasers and the Rebel's X-wings fire red lasers.

This black-and-white starfighter scarf is worked flat back and forth using the double knitting technique, creating a double-thick fabric where one side is the negative image of the other. Red and green laser detailing indicates which side each starfighter is on, whether it's the X-wing, TIE fighter, A-wing, TIE interceptor or Y-wing. Let the battle commence!

SIZE
One size

FINISHED MEASUREMENTS
Width: 16.5 cm / 6½ in.
Length: 175.5 cm / 69 in.

YARN
DK weight (light #3), shown in Oink Pigments *Mystic* (100% extrafine superwash merino wool; 210 m / 230 yd per 100 g / 3½ oz hank)
Colour A: The Dark Knitnight, 2 hanks
Colour B: Birthday Suit, 2 hanks
Colour C: REDRUM, 1 hank
Colour D: Three-Leaf Clover, 1 hank

NEEDLES
- 3.5 mm / US 4 needles or size needed to obtain tension

NOTION
- Tapestry needle

TENSION
22 sts and 29 rows = 10 cm / 4 in. in double knitting patt.
Be sure to check your tension.

NOTES
- This scarf is worked in two-colour double knitting; each row is worked with black (colour A) and one other colour. Be careful not to twist yarns when changing from front to back; the front and back should be distinct and separate layers, forming a tube.
- Weaving in ends as you go will make finishing easier.

Continued on page 88

SPECIAL TECHNIQUE
DOUBLE KNITTING

Double knitting is worked with twice as many stitches as are used for a single layer of knitting, creating two separate layers with knit stitches showing on each side of the work and the purl sides facing between both layers. Each square in the chart represents one pair of stitches: both the knit and the purl stitches. The knit stitch of the pair is worked using the colour shown in the chart, while the accompanying purl stitch of the pair is worked using the other colour. *Both* yarns are moved from back to front between needles for each stitch worked, creating two distinct layers of fabric with no floats.

Step 1: With both yarns at the back of the work, knit the first stitch of the pair with the colour shown in the chart.

Step 2: Bring both yarns to the front of the work between the two needles.

Step 3: With both yarns in front of the work, purl the second stitch of the pair with the colour not shown in the chart.

Step 4: Return both yarns to the back of the work between the needles.

Repeat Steps 1–4 for Double Knitting. When working 'WS' rows from the charts (those chart rows read from left to right), the colours are reversed. Use the colour not shown on the chart for the knit stitch of the pair, and the colour shown on the chart for the purl stitch of the pair.

SPECIAL TERM

Border Stitch (BS): Worked at the beginning of each row, hold both colours together and knit the first stitch of the front side and first stitch of the back side together. Worked at the end of each row, with both colours held together, knit the last stitch of the front side and last stitch of the back side together.

SCARF

With colours A and B held tog, CO 35
 sts – 70 loops on needle.
Arrange loops with colours alternating
 black loops in front and white loops
 in back.
Work *Rows 1–63 of Chart A, Rows
 64–122 of Chart B, Rows 123–186 of
 Chart C, then Rows 187–248 of Chart
 D; rep from * once more.
With both colours held tog, cast off all
 sts kwise, knitting each front st and
 corresponding back st tog as 1 st.

FINISHING

Weave in ends. Block if desired.

'STAY ON TARGET.'

–GOLD LEADER, *STAR WARS*: EPISODE IV *A NEW HOPE*

KEY

- ▨ A
- ☐ B
- ■ C
- ▨ D
- ⊞ Border st

CHART A

CHART B

KEY

KEY

- ◼ A
- ☐ B
- ◼ C
- ◼ D
- ⊞ Border st

CHART C

186
184
182
180
178
176
174
172
170
168
166
164
162
160
158
156
154
152
150
148
146
144
142
140
138
136
134
132
130
128
126
124

185
183
181
179
177
175
173
171
169
167
165
163
161
159
157
155
153
151
149
147
145
143
141
139
137
135
133
131
129
127
125
123

CHART D

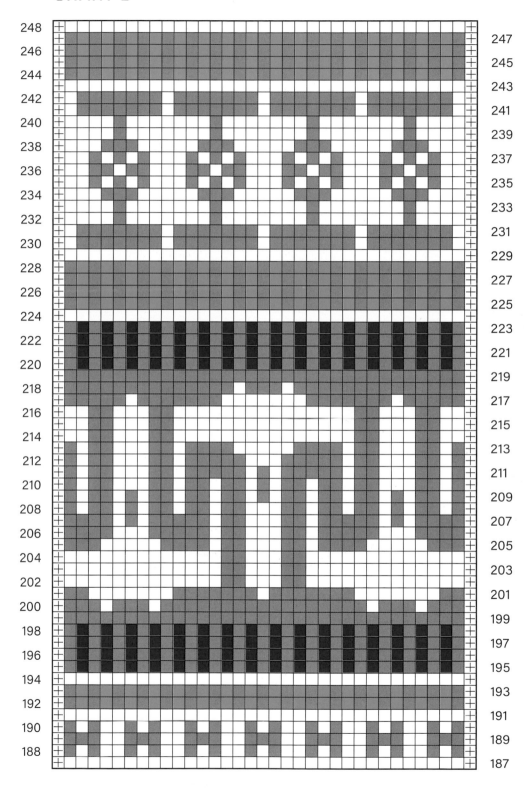

LIGHTSABER SOCKS

———— ▪►━━━ ————

Designed by: **CASSANDRA CRUIKSHANK**

LEVEL: ╱

No artifact is more closely associated with *Star Wars* than the lightsaber. Used in close combat, the lightsaber is an energy weapon that can block blaster shots and cut through almost anything. While all lightsabers have the same general design – kyber crystal core, pommel cap, hand grip, control panel, main hilt, focusing lens and blade emitter – certain features, especially the colour of the blade, make them unique to their bearer. Originally clear, the crystal changes colour when someone attuned to the Force awakens it.

Beginning with the lightsaber hilt, these over-the-knee tube socks are worked from the top down in the round. Ribbing in the cuff ensures they'll stay in place, while minimal leg shaping and lack of heel shaping allows for a multitude of sizes. The blade can be knit in any colour, leaving it up to the knitter to decide if they're a Jedi, a Sith or something in between.

SIZES

S (M, L)

Shown in size M.

Instructions are written for the smallest size, with larger sizes given in brackets; when only one number is given, it applies to all sizes.

FINISHED MEASUREMENTS

Foot Circumference: 16.5 (19, 21.5) cm / 6½ (7½, 8½) in.

Leg Circumference: 23 (26, 27.5) cm / 9 (10¼, 10¾) in.

YARN

3-ply weight (super fine #1) yarn, shown in SweetGeorgia *Tough Love Sock* (80% superwash merino, 20% nylon; 388 m / 425 yd per 115 g / 4 oz hank)

Colour A: Silver, 1 hank

Colour B: Cauldron, 1 hank

Colour C: Grape Jelly, 2 hanks

NEEDLES

- 2 mm / US 0, 100 cm / 40 in. long circular needle, or set of 4 or 5 double-pointed needles
- 2.25 mm / US 1, 100 cm / 40 in. long circular needle, or set of 4 or 5 double-pointed needles or size needed to obtain correct tension

NOTIONS

- Stitch markers
- Tapestry needle

TENSION

34 sts and 44 rnds = 10 cm / 4 in. in St st with larger needles

Be sure to check your tension.

Continued on page 96

LEG

With smaller needles and colour A, loosely CO 76 (88, 92) sts. Pm and join to work in the rnd, being careful not to twist sts.

Work 5 rnds in K1, P1 Rib.

Change to larger needles. Join colour B.

VERTICAL STRIPES

Setup rnd: *K2 A, k2 B; rep from * to end of rnd.

Next rnd: *K2 A, p2 B; rep from * to end of rnd.

Rep last rnd until piece measures approx 6.5 cm / 2½ in. Cut colour B.

With colour A, knit 1 rnd.

Work in K1, P1 Rib for 10 rnds.

Join colour B.

GARTER STRIPES

Knit 1 rnd with colour B.

Purl 1 rnd with colour B.

Knit 1 rnd with colour A.

Purl 1 rnd with colour A.

Rep last 4 rnds 2 more times, then work first 2 rnds with colour B again – 7 stripes total.

Cut colour B.

With colour A, knit 9 rnds, then purl 1 rnd.

Cut colour A.

Join colour C.

Work in St st until piece measures 23 cm / 9 in. from beg.

SHAPE LEG

Setup rnd: *K19 (22, 23), pm; rep from * to end of rnd.

Dec rnd: *K2tog, knit to marker; rep from * to end of rnd – 4 sts dec'd.

Knit 10 rnds even.

Rep last 11 rnds 4 (5, 4) more times – 56 (64, 72) sts rem. Remove all markers except beg-of-rnd marker.

Cont even until piece measures 2.5 (2.5, 3) cm / 1 (1, 1¼) in. less than desired length when worn as shown in photo.

SHAPE TOE

Dec rnd 1: *K5 (6, 7), k2tog; rep from * to end of rnd – 48 (56, 64) sts rem.

Knit 1 rnd even.

Dec rnd 2: *K4 (5, 6), k2tog; rep from * to end of rnd – 40 (48, 56) sts rem.

Knit 1 rnd even.

Dec rnd 3: *K3 (4, 5), k2tog; rep from * to end of rnd – 32 (40, 48) sts rem.

Knit 1 rnd even.

Dec rnd 4: *K2 (3, 4), k2tog; rep from * to end of rnd – 24 (32, 40) sts rem.

Knit 1 rnd even.

Dec rnd 5: *K1 (2, 3), k2tog; rep from * to end of rnd – 16 (24, 32) sts rem.

Knit 1 rnd even.

SIZES MEDIUM (LARGE) ONLY

Dec rnd 6: *K1 (2), k2tog; rep from * to end of rnd – 16 (24) sts rem.

SIZE L ONLY

Knit 1 rnd even.

Dec rnd 7: *K1, k2tog; rep from * to end of rnd – 16 sts rem.

ALL SIZES

Next dec rnd: *K2tog; rep from * to end of rnd – 8 sts rem.

Cut yarn, leaving a long tail. Thread tail through rem sts and pull tight to close hole. Secure on WS.

FINISHING

Weave in ends. Block to measurements.

'THIS IS THE WEAPON OF A JEDI KNIGHT. NOT AS CLUMSY OR RANDOM AS A BLASTER; AN ELEGANT WEAPON FOR A MORE CIVILISED AGE.'

—OBI-WAN KENOBI, *STAR WARS*: EPISODE IV *A NEW HOPE*

BEHIND THE SCENES:
Sound designer Ben Burtt accidentally invented the sound effect for the lightsabers in *A New Hope* when he recorded TV interference with a broken microphone.

TIE FIGHTER HAT AND MITTENS

⊢⊙⊣

Designed by: **BARBARA BENSON**

LEVEL: ///

Swift and agile with its twin ion engines, the TIE fighter is a staple in the Empire's fleet. With room for only one pilot, this ship lacks both hyperdrives and deflector shields, making it unable to travel long distances. Its black vertical wings collect solar energy, converting it into firepower that shoots from its two lasers. With its unique shape and deadly fighting capabilities, the TIE fighter is a terrifying reminder of the power of the Empire – and an unforgettable part of the *Star Wars* galaxy.

Knit from the bottom up in the round beginning with easy ribbing, the hat shifts into a slip-stitch colourwork pattern forming tiny TIE fighters. Once the colourwork is complete, the hat continues into spiralling crown decreases. The fingerless mitts are also worked from the bottom up in the round with matching ribbing and slip-stitch colourwork patterning. Formed with simple M1 increases, the thumb gusset works up quickly, while the remainder of the fingerless mitt is knit in a ribbed cast off, making this set perfect for space fighters everywhere.

SIZES

Hat: S (M/L, XL)

Shown in size S.

Instructions are written for the smallest size, with larger size given in brackets; when only one number is given, it applies to all sizes.

Fingerless Mitts: One size

FINISHED MEASUREMENTS

HAT

Circumference: 52 (57, 61.5) cm / 20½ (22½, 24¼) in.

Length: 21 (22, 23.5) cm / 8¼ (8¾, 9¼) in.

FINGERLESS MITTS

Hand Circumference: 17 cm / 6¾ in.

Length: 19.5 cm / 7¾ in.

YARN

3-ply weight (super fine #1) yarn, shown in Kim Dyes Yarn *Filo Sock* (80% superwash merino wool, 10% cashmere, 10% nylon; 366 m / 400 yd per 103 g / 3.6 oz hank)

Main Colour (MC): Silver Lining, 1 hank

Contrast Colour (CC): Pacifica, 1 hank

Note: One hank of each colour will make both hat and mitts.

NEEDLES

- 2.75 mm / US 2, 40 cm / 16 in. long circular needle, and set of 4 or 5 double-pointed needles or size needed to obtain correct tension
- 3.25 mm / US 3, 40 cm / 16 in. long circular needle, and set of 4 or 5 double-pointed needles or size needed to obtain correct tension

Continued on page 100

NOTIONS

- Stitch markers
- Stitch holders or waste yarn
- Tapestry needle
- Pom-pom maker

TENSIONS

30 sts and 41 rnds = 10 cm / 4 in. in St st with smaller needles

30 sts and 57 rnds = 10 cm / 4 in. in slip-stitch colourwork patt with larger needles

Be sure to check your tensions..

NOTES

- This pattern uses a variant of slip-stitch colourwork to mimic stranded knitting. You will only work with one strand of yarn at a time. Carry the unused yarn loosely up the inside of the piece, trapping the inactive yarn between the fabric and lifting the active yarn from below.
- The striping pattern is irregular; at times you are working single-row stripes and at other times more. The column at the left side of both charts tells you which colour is active; work with that colour only and do not carry the inactive colour along the row.
- Stitches are slipped purlwise with the yarn held at the back of work; make sure you keep yarn held at an even tension. There should be a bar of active yarn running horizontally behind the slipped stitches that is the width of those stitches. Do not pull tightly or the stitches will compact; do not allow the yarn to be too loose or the stitches on either side of the slipped stitches will elongate.

PATTERN STITCHES

K2, P2 Rib (multiple of 4 sts)

All rnds: *K2, p2; rep from * to end of rnd.

Stocking Stitch (any number of sts)

All rnds: Knit.

Tiny TIE A (multiple of 14 sts)

Rnds 1 and 9: With CC, *sl 2 wyib, (k1, sl 1 wyib) twice, k3, (sl 1 wyib, k1) twice, sl 1 wyib; rep from * to end of rnd.

Rnds 2 and 8: With MC, *k2, sl 1 wyib, k3, sl 3 wyib, k3, sl 1 wyib, k1; rep from * to end of rnd.

Rnds 3 and 7: With CC, *k1, sl 1 wyib, k1, sl 2 wyib, k5, sl 2 wyib, k1, sl 1 wyib; rep from * to end of rnd.

Rnds 4 and 6: With MC, *(k2, sl 1 wyib) twice, k3, sl 1 wyib, k2, sl 1 wyib, k1; rep from * to end of rnd.

Rnd 5: With CC, *sl 2 wyib, k4, sl 1 wyib, k1, sl 1 wyib, k4, sl 1 wyib; rep from * to end of rnd.

Tiny TIE B (multiple of 14 sts)

Rnds 1 and 9: With CC, *k2, (sl 1 wyib, k1) twice, sl 3 wyib, (k1, sl 1 wyib) twice, k1; rep from * to end of rnd.

Rnds 2 and 8: With MC, *sl 2 wyib, k3, (sl 1 wyib, k3) twice, sl 1 wyib; rep from * to end of rnd.

Rnds 3 and 7: With CC, *k3, sl 2 wyib, (k1, sl 1 wyib) twice, k1, sl 2 wyib, k2; rep from * to end of rnd.

Rnds 4 and 6: With MC, *(k2, sl 1 wyib) twice, k3, sl 1 wyib, k2, sl 1 wyib, k1; rep from * to end of rnd.

Rnd 5: With CC, *k1, sl 1 wyib, k4, sl 3 wyib, k4, sl 1 wyib; rep from * to end of rnd.

HAT

With smaller cir needle and CC, CO 152 (168, 180) sts using Long Tail method. Pm and join to work in the rnd, being careful not to twist sts.

Work in K2, P2 rib for 8 rnds.

Join MC.

SIZES S (XL) ONLY

Inc rnd: With MC, k38 (45), M1L, k76 (90), M1L, k38 (45) – 154 (182) sts.

Next rnd: With MC, knit.

SIZE M/L ONLY

Next 2 rnds: With MC, knit.

ALL SIZES

*Change to larger cir needle.

Work Rnds 1–9 of Tiny TIE A patt.

Change to smaller cir needle.

With MC, knit 2 rnds.

Change to larger cir needle.

Work Rnds 1–9 of Tiny TIE B patt.

Change to smaller cir needle.

With MC, knit 2 rnds.

Rep from * once more.

With CC, knit 2 rnds. Cut CC, leaving a long tail.

Cont with MC only in St st for 5 (7, 9) rnds.

SHAPE CROWN

Change to dpn when there are too few sts to work comfortably on cir needle.

Setup rnd: [K20 (22, 24), k2tog, pm] 6 times, k20 (22, 24), k2tog – 147 (161, 175) sts rem.

Next rnd: Knit even.

Dec Rnd: *Knit to 2 sts before marker, k2tog, sm; rep from * to end of rnd – 7 sts dec'd.

Rep last 2 rnds 9 more times – 77 (91, 105) sts rem.

Knit 1 rnd even.

Rep Dec rnd every rnd 10 (12, 14) times – 7 sts rem.

Cut yarn, leaving a long tail. Thread tail through rem sts and pull tight to close hole. Secure on WS.

FINISHING

Weave in ends. Block to finished measurements, being careful not to stretch out brim ribbing. Using CC, make pom-pom and attach to crown.

FINGERLESS MITTENS

With smaller dpn and CC, CO 56 sts using Long Tail method. Pm and join to work in the rnd, being careful not to twist sts.

Work in K2, P2 Rib for 4 rnds.

Join MC and knit 2 rnds.

Change to larger dpn.

Work Rnds 1–9 of Tiny TIE A patt.

Change to smaller dpn.

With MC, knit 2 rnds.

Change to larger dpn.

Work Rnds 1–9 of Tiny TIE B patt.

Change to smaller dpn.

With MC, knit 2 rnds.

With CC, knit 2 rnds. Cut CC, leaving a long tail.

Dec rnd: With MC, (k2tog, k16) twice, k2tog, k18 –53 sts rem.

Work even in St st for 8 rnds.

THUMB GUSSET

Setup (inc) rnd: K26, pm, M1L, pm, knit to end of rnd – 54 sts, with 1 st between markers for thumb gusset.

Knit 1 rnd even.

Inc rnd: Knit to marker, sm, M1L, knit to marker, M1R, sm, knit to end of rnd – 2 sts inc'd.

Rep Inc rnd every other rnd 6 more times, then every 3 rnds 3 times – 74 sts, with 21 sts between markers for thumb gusset.

Join CC and knit 2 rnds even.

With MC, rep Inc rnd again – 76 sts, with 23 sts between markers for thumb gusset.

Inc rnd: With MC, k1, M1L, k18, M1L, k7, sm, k23, sm, k11, M1L, k16 – 79 sts, with 23 sts between markers for thumb gusset.

DIVIDE HAND & THUMB

Change to larger dpn.

Next rnd: With CC, work Rnd 1 of Tiny TIE A patt to marker, remove marker, place 23 gusset sts on holder or waste yarn for thumb, remove marker, then cont in Tiny Tie A patt to end of rnd – 56 sts rem.

HAND

Work Rnds 2–9 of Tiny TIE A patt.

Change to smaller dpn.

With MC, knit 2 rnds.

Change to larger dpn.

Work Rnds 1–9 of Tiny TIE B patt.

Change to smaller dpn.

With MC, knit 2 rnds. Cut MC, leaving a long tail.

With CC, knit 1 rnd.

Work in K2, P2 Rib for 3 rnds.

With larger dpn, cast off loosely in patt.

THUMB

Return 23 held thumb gusset sts to smaller dpn.

Join MC, pick up and knit 2 sts in gap at top of thumb opening, then knit 23 gusset sts –25 sts. Arrange sts with 8 sts on 9 sts on first dpn, and 8 sts on each of rem 2 dpn. Pm and join to work in the rnd.

Dec rnd: K2tog, then knit to end of rnd – 24 sts rem.

Knit 2 rnds even. Cut yarn, leaving a long tail.

Join CC, and knit 1 rnd.

Work in K2, P2 Rib for 3 rnds.

With larger dpn, cast off loosely in patt.

Make second mitt to match.

FINISHING

Weave in ends, using tails at top of thumb gusset to close any holes. Block to finished measurements.

KEY

- ☐ MC
- ☐ CC
- ☐ knit
- ☑ sl 1 wyib
- ☐ repeat

CHART A

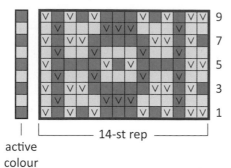

active
colour

14-st rep

CHART B

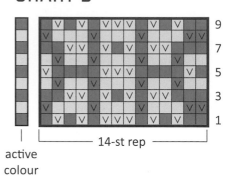

active
colour

14-st rep

BEHIND THE SCENES:
The TIE fighter's distinctive sound is an audio mix of bellowing elephants and cars driving in the rain.

THE *MILLENNIUM FALCON* COWL

Designed by: **RHIANA BAMS**

LEVEL: ///

First introduced in *A New Hope*, the *Millennium Falcon* is the legendary ship captained by Han Solo. Outfitted with smuggler's holds and heavily modified over the years, the *Millennium Falcon* is easily recognised by its distinctive shape and noted for its speed and agility. An asset to many of the characters fighting against the Empire and the First Order in the films, it is perhaps the most famous spaceship in cinema and holds a special place in the hearts of *Star Wars* fans everywhere.

Knit in the round in a tube, this unisex stranded-colourwork cowl begins with a provisional cast on. After the charts are worked, the ends are grafted together, creating a seamless loop. This cowl is knit in high-contrast colours with a sparkly accent yarn, making the *Falcon* look as if she is flying through twinkling stars in space.

SIZE
One size

FINISHED MEASUREMENTS
Circumference: 58.5 cm / 23 in.
Length: 80.5 cm / 31¾ in.

YARN
Colour A: DK weight (light #3) yarn, shown in The Lemonade Shop *Classic DK* (100% fine superwash merino; 211 m / 231 yd per 100 g / 4 oz hank), in colour The Dark Side, 2 hanks

Colour B: DK weight (light #3) yarn, shown in The Lemonade Shop *Sparkle DK* (75% superwash merino wool, 20% nylon, 5% metallic; 211 m / 231 yd per 100 g / 3½ oz hank), in colour The Light Side, 2 hanks

NEEDLES
• 3.75 mm / US 5, 40 cm / 16 in. long circular needle or size needed to obtain tension

NOTIONS
• Stitch markers
• Waste yarn
• Spare 3.75 mm / US 5, 40 cm / 16 in. long circular needle for Kitchener st join
• Tapestry needle

TENSION
26 sts and 23 rnds = 10 cm / 4 in. in chart patt
Be sure to check your tension.

Continued on page 108

- This cowl is worked in the round to form a tube using stranded colour knitting, beginning with a provisional cast on. Hold colour B as the dominant colour and weave in floats as needed, making sure you do not weave in at the same spot every round. The two ends are grafted together using Kitchener stitch.

COWL

With waste yarn, CO 150 sts using Long Tail method. Pm and join to work in the rnd, being careful not to twist sts. Knit 2 or 3 rnds. Cut waste yarn.

Join colours A and B.

Work Rnds 1–97 of Chart A.

Work Rnds 1–85 of Chart B.

Note: For a longer cowl, rep Chart B from Rnd 1; each 85-rnd rep should measure approx 37.5 cm / 14¾ in. long, but you'll need additional yarn for a longer cowl.

Cut colour B, leaving a long tail. Cut colour A, leaving a tail at least 2.75 m / 3 yd long, or 4 times the length of the rnd.

FINISHING

Weave in ends, except for tails at beg and colour A at end.

To remove provisional cast on, cut 1 waste yarn st at the end of the last waste yarn row, and place 150 sts from first row of cowl onto spare needle as waste yarn is removed.

Line up ends of cowl, making sure tube is not twisted. With long tail of colour A, join sts using Kitchener st.

Weave in rem ends. Block to measurements.

'FAST SHIP?... IT'S THE SHIP THAT MADE THE KESSEL RUN IN LESS THAN TWELVE PARSECS! ... SHE MAY NOT LOOK LIKE MUCH, BUT SHE'S GOT IT WHERE IT COUNTS, KID.'

—HAN SOLO, *STAR WARS*: EPISODE IV *A NEW HOPE*

CHART A

KEY ■ □

CHART B

A GALAXY FAR, FAR AWAY MITTENS

Designed by: **LOTTA LUNDIN**

LEVEL: ////

While every *Star Wars* film has had its share of iconic posters, the original poster for *A New Hope* is perhaps the most famous of all. Designed and painted by Tom Jung, with an alternate version painted by twin brothers Greg and Tim Hildebrandt in 1977, this bold composition helped the film attract a huge audience, converting the genre from niche to mainstream. Today, it remains one of the most recognisable film posters of all time.

Worked in the round from the cuff up, these traditionally shaped mittens are worked to a small tension, allowing for maximum detail. With a 2x2 twisted rib cuff, stranded colourwork creates two different scenes. Put the wearer's hands together and images from the original poster appear: Luke wielding a lightsaber, Darth Vader's sinister mask, the Death Star, and more create an action-packed scene on the outside of your hands! Flip them over and C-3PO, R2-D2 and other characters and artifacts from the *Star Wars* galaxy are hidden on the palm side. Afterthought thumbs and an optional third colour for the star are added after the tops of the mittens are grafted shut.

SIZE
One size

FINISHED MEASUREMENTS
Hand Circumference: 18.5 cm / 7¼ in.
Length: 26 cm / 10¼ in.

YARN
3-ply weight (super fine #1) yarn, shown in Emma's Yarn *Practically Perfect Sock* (80% superwash merino wool, 20% nylon; 366 m / 400 yd. per 100 g / 3½ oz hank)
Main Colour (MC): Denim, 1 hank
Contrast Colour (CC): Jackie O, 1 hank

NEEDLES
• 2 mm / US 0, set of 5 doubled-pointed needles or size needed to obtain correct tension

NOTIONS
• Stitch markers
• Stitch holders or waste yarn
• 13.75 m / 15 yd of 3-ply weight (super fine #1) yarn in yellow
• Tapestry needle

TENSION
44 sts and 45 rnds = 10 cm / 4 in. in chart patt
Be ure to check your tension.

Continued on page 114

NOTES

- These mittens are worked in the round on double-pointed needles. You may choose to use one long circular needle and the Magic Loop method, or two short circular needles.
- The yellow accents in these mittens can be knit into the pattern as you work, or knit those stitches with CC, then add the yellow using duplicate stitch when the mittens are complete.

PATTERN STITCH

Beaded Rib (multiple of 5 sts)

Rnd 1: *K3, p2; rep from * to end of rnd.

Rnd 2: *K1, p1, k1, p2; rep from * to end of rnd.

Rep Rnds 1 and 2 for patt.

LEFT MITTEN
CUFF

With colour A, Co 65 sts. Divide sts over 4 dpn with 15 sts each on Needles 1, 2 and 3, and 20 sts on Needle 4. Pm and join to work in the rnd, being careful not to twist sts.

Rnd 1: *K1-tbl; rep from * to end of rnd.

Work in Beaded Rib until cuff measures approx 5 cm / 2 in. .

Inc rnd 1: *K13, M1; rep from * to end of rnd – 70 sts.

Inc rnd 2: K7, *M1, k14; rep from * 3 more times, M1, then knit to end of rnd – 75 sts.

Inc rnd 3: K10, *M1, k15; rep from * 3 more times, M1, then knit to end of rnd – 80 sts.

Knit 1 rnd even. Redistribute sts over dpn with 20 sts on each needle. Pm after 40 sts.

HAND

Join CC.
Work Rnds 1–31 of Left Mitten chart.

THUMB HOLE

Next rnd: Work first 26 sts of Rnd 32, place next 13 sts on holder or waste yarn, CO 13 sts with MC over opening using Backward Loop method, then work to end of rnd.
Cont even in patt through Rnd 71 of chart.

SHAPE TOP

Dec rnd: Working next rnd of chart, *k2, ssk, work to 3 sts before marker, k2tog, k1; rep from * once more – 4 sts dec'd.
Rep last rnd 15 more times – 16 sts rem. Cut CC.
Slip 4 sts from Needle 2 to Needle 1 and 4 sts from Needle 3 to Needle 4. With MC, graft sts tog using Kitchener st.

THUMB

With RS facing, return 13 held sts to dpn. With MC, pick up and knit 2 sts in gap at side of thumb hole, 13 sts along CO sts above opening, then 2 sts in gap at side of thumb hole – 30 sts.
Distribute sts over 4 dpn with 7 sts each on Needles 1 and 3 and 8 sts on Needles 2 and 4. Pm and join to work in the rnd, beg rnds at edge closest to palm.
Work Rnds 1–21 of Thumb chart. On Rnd 21, pm after 15 sts.

SHAPE TOP

Dec rnd: Working next rnd of chart, *k1, ssk, work to 3 sts before marker, k2tog, k1; rep from * once more – 4 sts dec'd.
Rep last rnd 4 more times –10 sts rem.
Cut CC. Cut MC, leaving a long tail. Thread tail through rem sts and pull tight to close hole. Secure on WS.

RIGHT MITTEN
CUFF

Work same as Left Mitten.

HAND

Join CC.
Work Rnds 1–31 of Right Mitten chart.

THUMB HOLE

Next rnd: Place first 13 sts on holder or waste yarn, CO 13 sts with MC over opening using Backward Loop method, then work to end of rnd.
Cont even in patt through Rnd 71 of chart.

SHAPE TOP

Dec rnd: Working next rnd of chart, *k2, ssk, work to 3 sts before marker, k2tog, k1; rep from * once more – 4 sts dec'd.
Rep last rnd 15 more times –16 sts rem. Cut CC.
Slip 4 sts from Needle 2 to Needle 1 and 4 sts from Needle 3 to Needle 4. With MC, graft sts tog using Kitchener st.

THUMB

Work same as Left Mitten.

FINISHING

Weave in ends. Block to measurements.

KEY

- ■ MC
- □ CC
- ▨ knit with yellow or knit with CC, then add yellow using duplicate st
- ▨ k2tog
- ▨ ssk
- ▬ thumb hole

THUMB CHART

LEFT MITTEN CHART

RIGHT MITTEN CHART

CHANCELLOR PALPATINE SCARF

Designed by: **TANIS GRAY**

LEVEL: ✎

Chancellor Palpatine's true colours finally emerge in *Revenge of the Sith*, as we see him transform from a regally dressed Senate leader and concerned politician into the sinister and loathsome Darth Sidious. Hiding his true nature as a Sith for many years, Palpatine uses his position on the Senate to manipulate events in his favour, ultimately reshaping the Galactic Republic into the evil Empire and turning promising Jedi Anakin Skywalker to the dark side. Cruel, power hungry and arrogant, the sleek Chancellor is the ultimate villain of the *Star Wars* saga.

Worked flat the long way to mimic the silken woven fabric of Chancellor Palpatine's over tunic, this unisex cabled scarf is a straightforward and easy-to-memorise eight-row pattern repeat. The intertwined texture of the cable combined with the ruby red make this a luscious, opulent knit for anyone seeking to show off their power.

SIZES
One size

FINISHED MEASUREMENTS
Width: 18.5 cm / 7¼ in.
Length: 223 cm / 87¾ in.

YARN
Aran weight (medium #4) yarn, shown in Katia/KFI *Concept Cotton-Merino* (70% cotton, 30% extrafine merino wool; 105 m / 115 yd per 50 g / 1¾ oz ball) in colour #53 Crimson, 6 balls

NEEDLES
- 4 mm / US 6, 150 cm / 60 in. long circular needle
- 5 mm / US 8, 150 cm / 60 in. long circular needle or size needed to obtain tension

NOTIONS
- Stitch markers
- Cable needle
- Tapestry needle

TENSION
18½ sts and 30 rows = 10 cm / 4 in. in cable patt on larger needles
Make sure to check your tension.

NOTES
- Scarf is knit back and forth in rows across the length. Garter-stitch bands on both long edges are worked on smaller needles; the cabled body is worked on larger needles.
- It may be helpful to place markers between each chart repeat.

Continued on page 122

SPECIAL TERMS

1/1 LC (1 over 1 left cross): Sl 1 st to cn and hold at front, k1, then k1 from cn.

1/1 LPC (1 over 1 left purl cross): Sl 1 st to cn and hold at front, p1, then k1 from cn.

1/1 RC (1 over 1 right cross): Sl 1 st to cn and hold at back, k1, then k1 from cn.

1/1 RPC (1 over 1 right purl cross): Sl 1 st to cn and hold at back, k1, then p1 from cn.

PATTERN STITCH

Cable Pattern (multiple of 8 sts + 6)

Row 1 (RS): K3, *1/1 RPC, p1, 1/1 RC, p1, 1/1 LPC; rep from * to last 3 sts, k3.

Row 2 (WS): K3, *p1, k2, p2, k2, p1; rep from * to last 3 sts, k3.

Row 3: K3, *k1, p2, 1/1 RC, p2, k1; rep from * to last 3 sts, k3.

Row 4: Rep Row 2.

Row 5: K3, *1/1 LPC, 1/1 RC, 1/1 LC, 1/1 RPC; rep from * to last 3 sts, k3.

Row 6: K3, *k1, p6, k1; rep from * to last 3 sts, k3.

Row 7: K3, *p1, 1/1 RPC, 1/1 RC, 1/1 LPC, p1; rep from * to last 3 sts, k3.

Row 8: K3, *k1, p1, k1, p2, k1, p1, k1; rep from * to last 3 sts, k3.

Rep Rows 1–8 for patt.

SCARF

With smaller cir needle, CO 406 sts using Long Tail method. Do not join.
Knit 4 rows (2 garter ridges).
Change to larger cir needle.
Work Rows 1–8 of Cable patt 6 times.
Change to smaller cir needle.
Knit 3 rows.
With larger needle, cast off kwise.

FINISHING

Weave in ends. Block to measurements.

'THE DARK SIDE
OF THE FORCE IS
A PATHWAY TO
MANY ABILITIES
SOME CONSIDER TO
BE UNNATURAL.'

–CHANCELLOR PALPATINE,
STAR WARS: EPISODE III
REVENGE OF THE SITH

CABLE CHART

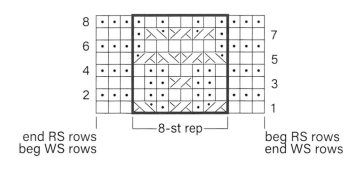

8-st rep

end RS rows
beg WS rows

beg RS rows
end WS rows

KEY

☐ k on RS, p on WS

⊡ p on RS, k on WS

⧄ 1/1 LC

⧄ 1/1 LPC

⧄ 1/1 RC

⧄ 1/1 RPC

☐ pattern repeat

GENERAL LEIA ORGANA PULLOVER

Designed by: **CARISSA BROWNING**

LEVEL: ///

In *The Force Awakens*, Princess Leia has become General Leia Organa, leader of the Resistance – a ragtag group of rebels determined to quash the rise of the First Order. With her strong personality, ability to formulate a plan, excellent leadership and calm demeanour, Leia is a natural leader. As general, Leia becomes a symbol of hope and perseverance for the Resistance, even after her death in *The Rise of Skywalker*.

Knit in the round from the bottom up to the armholes in stocking stitch, this pullover – inspired by the stunning sapphire robe worn by Leia in Episode VII *The Force Awakens* – is then divided so that the front and back can be worked flat separately. Gradual decreases near the waist create a subtle and flattering A-line silhouette, while German short row shaping is used for a better fit in the shoulders. The sleeves begin in the round, then are worked flat for sleeve cap shaping. The notched collar is picked up and worked at the end.

SIZES

XS (S, M, L, XL, 2XL, 3XL, 4XL, 5XL, 6XL, 7XL)

Shown in size S.

Instructions are written for the smallest size, with larger sizes given in brackets; when only one number is given, it applies to all sizes.

FINISHED MEASUREMENTS

Bust: 83 (92, 101.5, 112.5, 122, 131.5, 140.5, 152, 160.5, 170, 179) cm / 32¾ (36¼, 40, 44¼, 48, 51¾, 55¼, 59¾, 63¼, 67, 70½) in.

Length: 59 (61.5, 63, 66.5, 68, 70.5, 73, 75.5, 77, 78, 78) cm / 23¼ (24¼, 24¾, 26¼, 26¾, 27¾, 28¾, 29¾, 30¼, 30¾, 30¾) in.

YARN

DK weight (light #3) yarn, shown in Anzula Yarns *Cricket* (80% superwash merino, 10% cashmere, 10% nylon; 228 m / 250 yd per 114 g / 4 oz hank), in colour Storm, 5 (5, 6, 6, 7, 7, 8, 8, 9, 9, 10) hanks

NEEDLES

• 3.75 mm / US 5 , 40 cm / 16 in. and 80 cm / 32 in. long circular needles, and set of 4 or 5 double-pointed needles or size needed to obtain correct tension

NOTIONS

• Stitch markers
• Stitch holders or waste yarn
• Spare 3.75 mm / US 5 needle for Three-Needle Cast Off
• Tapestry needle

Continued on page 128

TENSION

22 sts and 30 rnds/rows = 10 cm / 4 in. in St st

Be sure to check your tension.

NOTES

- The body of this pullover is worked in the round from the bottom up to the armholes, then divided to work the front and back flat. The garter-stitch neck placket begins after armhole decreases are complete.

- An Italian cast on is used for a clean edge and stretchy hem and cuffs. German short rows are used to shape the shoulders for a better fit.

SPECIAL TECHNIQUE
ITALIAN CAST ON

Make a slipknot with the yarn, leaving a tail long enough to cast on the required number of stitches (usually about 2.5 cm / 1 in. per stitch), and place the slipknot on the needle.

Holding the needle in your right hand, hold both strands of yarn in your left hand as for a Long Tail cast on, with the long tail over your index finger and the end coming from the ball over your thumb.

*Spread your thumb and index finger apart to form a V.

Insert the needle tip down behind the strand on your index finger, bring it forwards under both strands, up in front of the strand on your thumb, and down between the two strands, then bring the needle tip up behind the back strand – 1 purl stitch cast on.

Insert the needle tip down in front of the strand on your thumb, back under the front strand and up between the two strands, bring it over the top and down behind the strand on your index finger, forwards under both strands, then bring needle tip up in front of the front strand –1 knit stitch cast on.

Repeat from * until the required number of stitches have been cast on, ending with a purl stitch.

PATTERN STITCHES

K1, P1 Rib (even number of sts)

All rnds: *K1, p1; rep from * for patt.

Stocking Stitch (any number of sts)

Worked back and forth, knit RS rows, purl WS rows.

Worked in the rnd, knit every rnd.

Garter Stitch (any number of sts)

Worked back and forth, knit every row.

Worked in the rnd, *Knit 1 rnd, purl 1 rnd; rep from * for patt.

BODY

With longer cir needle, CO 200 (220, 240, 264, 284, 304, 324, 348, 368, 388, 408) sts using Italian CO method.

Setup row 1 (RS): *K1, sl 1 wyif; rep from * to end.

Setup row 2 (WS): *K1, sl 1 wyif; rep from * to end.

Pm and join to work in the rnd, being careful not to twist sts.

Work in K1, P1 Rib for 4 cm / 1½ in.

Setup rnd 3: K18 (20, 22, 24, 26, 28, 30, 32, 34, 36, 38), pm, k64 (70, 76, 84, 90, 96, 102, 110, 116, 122, 128), pm, k36 (40, 44, 48, 52, 56, 60, 64, 68, 72, 76), pm, k64 (70, 76, 84, 90, 96, 102, 110, 116, 122, 128), pm, k18 (20, 22, 24, 26, 28, 30, 32, 34, 36, 38).

Work in St st until piece measures 6.5 cm / 2½ in.

Dec rnd: *Knit to marker, sm, ssk, knit to 2 sts before next marker, k2tog, sm; rep from * to end – 4 sts dec'd.

Knit 10 (11, 11, 12, 12, 13, 13, 14, 14, 14, 14) rnds even.

Rep last 11 (12, 12, 13, 13, 14, 14, 15, 15, 15, 15) rnds 4 more times – 180 (200, 220, 244, 264, 284, 304, 328, 348, 368, 388) sts rem.

Remove dart markers and pm after 90 (100, 110, 122, 132, 142, 152, 164, 174, 184, 194) sts.

Work in St st until body measures 38.5 (40, 40, 41.5, 41.5, 42.5, 42.5, 44, 44, 44, 44) cm / 15¼ (15¾, 15¾, 16¼, 16¼, 16¾, 16¾, 17¼, 17¼, 17¼, 17¼) in. from CO edge, ending last rnd 7 (8, 10, 12, 14, 16, 18, 20, 22, 24, 26) sts before end of rnd.

DIVIDE FRONT AND BACK

Next rnd: Cast off 14 (16, 20, 24, 28, 32, 36, 40, 44, 48, 52) sts, knit to 7 (8, 10, 12, 14, 16, 18, 20, 22, 24, 26) sts before next marker, cast off 14 (16, 20, 24, 28, 32, 36, 40, 44, 48, 52) sts, then knit to end of rnd – 76 (84, 90, 98, 104, 110,

"REY . . . MAY THE FORCE BE WITH YOU."

—GENERAL LEIA ORGANA, *STAR WARS*: EPISODE VII *THE FORCE AWAKENS*

116, 124, 130, 136, 142) sts rem each for front and back. Place front sts on holder or waste yarn.

BACK

Next row (WS): Purl.

Dec row (RS): K2, ssk, knit to last 4 sts, k2tog, k2 – 2 sts dec'd.

Rep last 2 rows 4 (4, 5, 7, 8, 9, 10, 12, 13, 14, 15) more times – 66 (74, 78, 82, 86, 90, 94, 98, 102, 106, 110) sts rem.

Cont even until armhole measures 17 (18.5, 19.5, 21.5, 23, 23.5, 26, 27.5, 28.5, 30, 30) cm / 6¾ (7¼, 7¾, 8½, 9, 9¼, 10¼, 10¾, 11¼, 11¾, 11¾) in., ending with a WS row.

SHAPE NECK

Next row (RS): K20 (23, 24, 25, 26, 28, 29, 31, 31, 33, 34), join a second ball of yarn and cast off next 26 (28, 30, 32, 34, 34, 36, 36, 40, 40, 42) sts for neck, then knit to end –20 (23, 24, 25, 26, 28, 29, 31, 31, 33, 34) sts rem for each side.

Working each side at the same time with separate balls of yarn, work 1 WS row even.

Dec row (RS): Knit to 4 sts before neck, k2tog, k2; other side, k2, ssk, knit to end of row – 1 st dec'd each side of neck.

Rep last 2 rows 1 (1, 1, 2, 2, 3, 3, 3, 3, 3, 3) more time(s) –18 (21, 22, 22, 23, 24, 25, 27, 27, 29, 30) sts rem.

Place rem sts for right shoulder on holder or waste yarn.

SHAPE SHOULDERS
LEFT SHOULDER

Purl 1 row.

Short Row 1 (RS): K12 (14, 15, 15, 15, 16, 17, 18, 18, 19, 20), turn.

Short Row 2 (WS): Sl 1 pwise wyif, pull yarn tightly up and over RH needle to create a double st (DS), bring yarn to front between needles, then purl to end of row.

Short Row 3: K6 (7, 7, 7, 8, 8, 8, 9, 9, 10, 10), turn.

Short Row 4: DS, then purl to end of row.

Next row: Knit to end of row, and knit both legs of each DS tog.

Place sts on holder or waste yarn.

RIGHT SHOULDER

Return 18 (21, 22, 22, 23, 24, 25, 27, 27, 29, 30) held sts for right shoulder to shorter cir needle. Join yarn to beg with a WS row.

Short Row 1 (WS): P12 (14, 15, 15, 15, 16, 17, 18, 18, 19, 20), turn.

Short Row 2 (RS): Bring yarn to front between needles, sl 1 pwise wyif, pull yarn tightly up and over RH needle to create DS, then knit to end of row.

Short Row 3: P6 (7, 7, 7, 8, 8, 8, 9, 9, 10, 10), turn.

Short Row 4: DS, then knit to end of row.

Next row: Purl to end of row and purl both legs of each DS tog.

Next row: Knit.

Place sts on holder or waste yarn.

FRONT

Return 76 (84, 90, 98, 104, 110, 116, 124, 130, 136, 142) held front sts to longer cir needle.

Rejoin yarn to beg with a WS row.

Next row (WS): Purl.

Dec row (RS): K2, ssk, knit to last 4 sts, k2tog, k2 –2 sts dec'd.

Rep last 2 rows 4 (4, 5, 7, 8, 9, 10, 12, 13, 14, 15) more times, ending with a RS row –66 (74, 78, 82, 86, 90, 94, 98, 102, 106, 110) sts.

BEGIN PLACKET

Next row (WS): P32 (36, 38, 40, 42, 44, 46, 48, 50, 52, 54), pm, k2, pm, then purl to end of row.

Next row (RS): Knit to 2 sts before marker, k2tog, sm, M1L, knit to marker, M1R, sm, ssk, then knit to end of row.

Next row: Purl to marker, sm, knit to marker, sm, then purl to end of row.

Work 9 more rows as established –14 sts between markers in garter st.

SHAPE NECK

Row 1 (WS): Purl to marker, sm, k6, sl 1 wyif, join a second ball of yarn, k7, sm, then purl to end of row –33 (37, 39, 41, 43, 45, 47, 49, 51, 53, 55) sts for each side.

Row 2 (RS): Knit to marker, sm, k6, sl 1 wyif; other side, knit to marker, sm, then knit to end of row.

Row 3: Purl to marker, sm, k6, sl 1 wyif; other side, k7, sm, then purl to end of row.

Row 4 (dec): Knit to 2 sts before marker, k2tog, sm, k6, sl 1 wyif; other side, k7, sm, ssk, then knit to end of row—1 st dec'd each side.

Rep Dec row every 4 rows 4 (5, 5, 6, 6, 6, 7, 7, 7, 7, 8) more times –28 (31, 33, 34, 36, 38, 39, 41, 43, 45, 46) sts rem for each side.

Work 1 WS row even.

Next row (RS): Knit to marker, sm, k6, sl 1 wyif; other side, cast off 7 (7, 8, 8, 9, 9, 9, 9, 10, 10, 10) sts, then knit to end of row.

Next row: Purl to neck edge; other side, cast off 7 (7, 8, 8, 9, 9, 9, 9, 10, 10, 10) sts, then purl to end of row – 21 (24, 25, 26, 27, 29, 30, 32, 33, 35, 36) sts rem for each side.

Dec row: Knit to 4 sts before neck edge, k2tog, k2; other side, k2, ssk, then knit to end of row – 1 st dec'd each side.

Purl 1 row even.

Rep last 2 rows 2 (2, 2, 3, 3, 4, 4, 4, 5, 5, 5) more times –18 (21, 22, 22, 23, 24, 25, 27, 27, 29, 30) sts rem for each side.

Cont even until armhole measures 18.5 (19.5, 21, 23.5, 25, 26, 28.5, 30, 31, 32.5, 32.5) cm / 7¼ (7¾, 8¼, 9¼, 9¾, 10¼, 11¼, 11¾, 12¼, 12¾, 12¾) in., ending with a WS row.

SHAPE SHOULDERS

Shape shoulders same as back.

Join shoulders using Three-Needle Cast Off.

SLEEVES

With shorter cir needle, CO 40 (42, 44, 46, 48, 50, 52, 52, 54, 56, 58) sts using Italian CO method.

Setup row 1 (RS): *K1, sl 1 wyif; rep from * to end.

Setup row 2 (WS): *K1, sl1 wyif; rep from * to end.

Change to dpn. Pm and join to work in the rnd, being careful not to twist sts.

Work in K1, P1 Rib until piece measures 4.5 cm / 1¾ in.

Knit 8 (7, 6, 6, 5, 5, 4, 4, 4, 3, 3) rnds.

Inc rnd: K2, M1L, knit to last 2 sts, M1R, k2 –2 sts inc'd.

Rep Inc rnd every 9 (8, 7, 7, 6, 6, 5, 5, 5, 4, 4) rnds 11 (12, 14, 15, 17, 19, 10, 23, 24, 13, 14) more times, then every 0 (0, 0, 0, 0, 0, 6, 0, 0, 5, 5) rnds 0 (0, 0, 0, 0, 0, 10, 0, 0, 13, 13) times –64 (68, 74, 78, 84, 90, 94, 100, 104, 110, 114) sts.

Cont even until sleeve measures 45 (45, 46.5, 46.5, 47.5, 49, 48.5, 48.5, 48.5, 48.5, 48.5) cm / 17¾ (17¾, 18¼, 18¼, 18¾, 19¼, 19, 19, 19, 19, 19) in. from beg, ending last rnd 6 (7, 9, 11, 13, 15, 17, 19, 21, 23, 25) sts before end of rnd.

SHAPE CAP

Next rnd: Cast off 12 (14, 18, 22, 26, 30, 34, 38, 42, 46, 50) sts, then knit to end of rnd –52 (54, 56, 56, 58, 60, 60, 62, 62, 64, 64) sts rem.

Work 1 (3, 3, 3, 3, 3, 3, 3, 3, 3, 3) row(s), ending with a WS row.

Dec row (RS): K2, ssk, knit to last 4 sts, k2tog, k2 –2 sts dec'd.

Rep Dec row every 4 rows 0 (2, 1, 4, 4, 6, 6, 6, 6, 6, 6) more time(s), then every RS row 16 (14, 16, 12, 13, 11, 11, 11, 11, 11, 11) more times – 18 (20, 20, 22, 22, 24, 24, 26, 26, 28, 28) sts rem.

Cast off 2 sts at beg of next 4 rows –10 (12, 12, 14, 14, 16, 16, 18, 18, 20, 20) sts rem.

Cast off rem sts.

FINISHING

Weave in ends. Block pieces to measurements.

Sew in sleeves.

COLLAR

With shorter cir needle and RS facing, beg at upper right corner of front neck above garter st placket (see photo for reference), pick up and knit 1 st in each row along right neck, 26 (28, 30, 32, 34, 34, 36, 36, 40, 40, 42) sts along cast-off edge of back neck, then 1 st in each row along left neck, ending above garter st placket –approx 84 (86, 92, 98, 104, 110, 116, 116, 124, 128, 132) sts. Do not join.

Row 1 (WS): Sl 1 wyif, knit to last st evenly dec'ing approx 14 (14, 15, 16, 17, 18, 19, 19, 20, 21, 22) sts or number of sts required to get to rem number of sts, then sl 1 st wyif –70 (72, 77, 82, 87, 92, 97, 97, 104, 107, 110) sts rem.

Row 2 (RS): Knit to last st, sl 1 wyif.

Rep last row 8 more times.

Cast off all sts kwise.

Weave in rem ends.

CHARTS

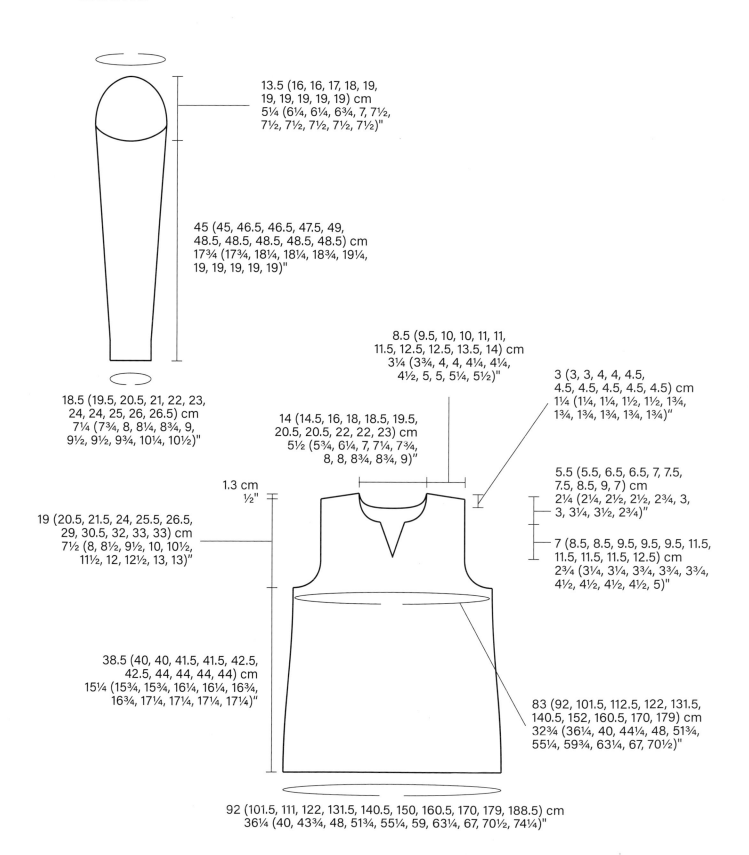

13.5 (16, 16, 17, 18, 19,
19, 19, 19, 19, 19) cm
5¼ (6¼, 6¼, 6¾, 7, 7½,
7½, 7½, 7½, 7½, 7½)"

45 (45, 46.5, 46.5, 47.5, 49,
48.5, 48.5, 48.5, 48.5, 48.5) cm
17¾ (17¾, 18¼, 18¼, 18¾, 19¼,
19, 19, 19, 19, 19)"

8.5 (9.5, 10, 10, 11, 11,
11.5, 12.5, 12.5, 13.5, 14) cm
3¼ (3¾, 4, 4, 4¼, 4¼,
4½, 5, 5, 5¼, 5½)"

3 (3, 3, 4, 4, 4.5,
4.5, 4.5, 4.5, 4.5, 4.5) cm
1¼ (1¼, 1¼, 1½, 1½, 1¾,
1¾, 1¾, 1¾, 1¾, 1¾)"

18.5 (19.5, 20.5, 21, 22, 23,
24, 24, 25, 26, 26.5) cm
7¼ (7¾, 8, 8¼, 8¾, 9,
9½, 9½, 9¾, 10¼, 10½)"

14 (14.5, 16, 18, 18.5, 19.5,
20.5, 20.5, 22, 22, 23) cm
5½ (5¾, 6¼, 7, 7¼, 7¾,
8, 8, 8¾, 8¾, 9)"

5.5 (5.5, 6.5, 6.5, 7, 7.5,
7.5, 8.5, 9, 7) cm
2¼ (2¼, 2½, 2½, 2¾, 3,
3, 3¼, 3½, 2¾)"

1.3 cm
½"

19 (20.5, 21.5, 24, 25.5, 26.5,
29, 30.5, 32, 33, 33) cm
7½ (8, 8½, 9½, 10, 10½,
11½, 12, 12½, 13, 13)"

7 (8.5, 8.5, 9.5, 9.5, 9.5, 11.5,
11.5, 11.5, 11.5, 12.5) cm
2¾ (3¼, 3¼, 3¾, 3¾, 3¾,
4½, 4½, 4½, 4½, 5)"

38.5 (40, 40, 41.5, 41.5, 42.5,
42.5, 44, 44, 44, 44) cm
15¼ (15¾, 15¾, 16¼, 16¼, 16¾,
16¾, 17¼, 17¼, 17¼, 17¼)"

83 (92, 101.5, 112.5, 122, 131.5,
140.5, 152, 160.5, 170, 179) cm
32¾ (36¼, 40, 44¼, 48, 51¾,
55¼, 59¾, 63¼, 67, 70½)"

92 (101.5, 111, 122, 131.5, 140.5, 150, 160.5, 170, 179, 188.5) cm
36¼ (40, 43¾, 48, 51¾, 55¼, 59, 63¼, 67, 70½, 74¼)"

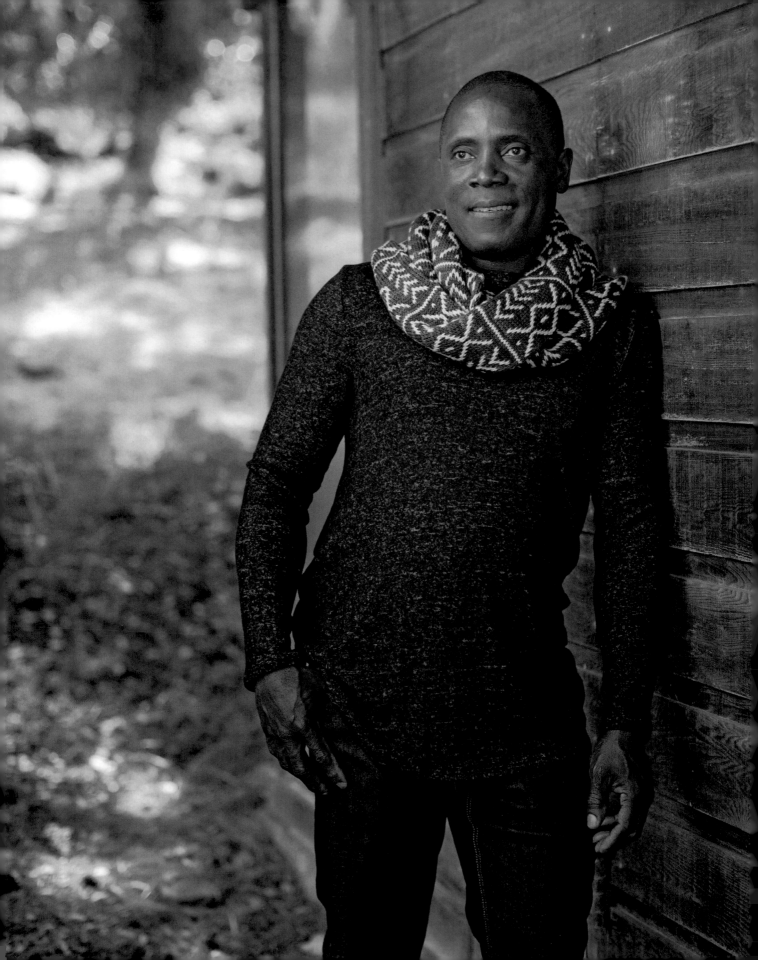

ANAKIN'S INFINITY COWL

Designed by: **TANIS GRAY**

LEVEL: ///

Growing up on the harsh desert planet of Tatooine in *The Phantom Menace*, Anakin Skywalker and his mother, Shmi, are slaves who belong to the winged Toydarian, Watto. From an early age, Anakin demonstrates his intelligence and his love of creating things, often making droids or helpful tools to assist his mother and master. His room is a collection of machine parts, half-finished projects and trinkets he has collected, including a cushion with a distinctive pattern. The same pattern is later seen in Episode II *Attack of the Clones* as part of his costume when he and Padmé flee the Capital to lie low on Naboo.

Inspired by Anakin's unique textiles, this unisex stranded colourwork cowl starts with a provisional cast on and is then knit in the round from the bottom up in a tube. The simple Fair Isle pattern works up quickly, and the length is easily adjustable. The ends are not cast off but instead grafted together, creating a seamless loop.

SIZE
One size

FINISHED MEASUREMENTS
Width: 37 cm / 14½ in.
Circumference: 178 cm / 70 in.

YARN
Aran weight (medium #4) yarn, shown in Queen City Yarn *Wesley Heights Worsted* (100% superwash merino wool; 199 m / 218 yd per 100 g / 3½ oz hank)
Colour A: He'll Only Wear Black Socks, 3 hanks
Colour B: Pants with Pleats, 2 hanks

NEEDLES
- 4.5 mm / US 7, 40 cm / 16 in. long circular needle or size needed to obtain correct tension

NOTIONS
- Stitch markers
- Waste yarn
- 4 mm / US G-6 crochet hook
- Spare 4.5 mm / US 7 needle
- Tapestry needle

TENSION
24 sts and 20 rnds = 10 cm / 4 in. in chart patt
Be sure to check your tension.

NOTES
- Cowl is worked in the round from the bottom up, starting with a provisional cast on. After stranded colourwork is complete, the stitches from both ends are joined using Kitchener stitch.

COWL

With colour A, CO 88 sts using Chained
Provisional CO. Pm and join to work in
the rnd, being careful not to twist sts.
Work Rnds 1–50 of Chart 6 times, then
work Rnds 1–49 again.
Cut colour A.

FINISHING

Weave in ends. Block to
measurements.
Remove provisional CO and place
resulting 88 sts on spare cir needle.
With colour B, join ends using
Kitchener st.

CHART

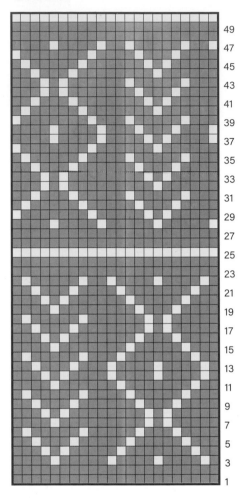

- ■ A
- □ B
- ☐ repeat

PADMÉ AMIDALA:

'YOU'RE NOT
ALL-POWERFUL, ANI.'

ANAKIN SKYWALKER:

'WELL, I SHOULD BE.'

—*STAR WARS*: EPISODE II
ATTACK OF THE CLONES

YODA MITTS

Designed by: **CARISSA BROWNING**

LEVEL: ///

Though small in stature and 900 years old, Jedi Master Yoda is an extraordinarily powerful, wise and fearless warrior. A member of an unknown species with green skin, he has large pointy ears and three-fingered claws. With his green lightsaber at his side, Yoda may be small, but he is fierce.

Worked from the cuff up primarily in seed stitch, centre double increases along one edge form the thumb gusset, which is placed on waste yarn while the palm is completed. Palm stitches are divided to form the fingers, which are worked individually then topped with cream-coloured yarn worked in stocking stitch to form claws. Multiple sizing for children 1 to 12 years ensures the perfect fit for even the tiniest Yoda fans.

SIZES

0–1 year (1–2 years, 2–4 years, 4–6 years, 6–8 years, 8–12 years)

Shown in size 2–4 years.

Instructions are written for the smallest size, with larger sizes given in brackets; when only one number is given, it applies to all sizes.

FINISHED MEASUREMENTS

Hand Circumference: 11 (12.5, 13.5, 15, 16, 18) cm / 4¼ (5, 5¼, 6, 6¼, 7) in.

Length: 11.5 (14, 16.5, 18.5, 19.5, 21.5) cm / 4½ (5½, 6½, 7¼, 7¾, 8½) in.

YARN

Aran weight (medium #4) yarn, shown in Berroco *Vintage* (52% acrylic, 40% wool, 8% nylon; 199 m / 218 yd per 100 g / 3½ oz hank)

Colour A: #5175 Fennel, 1 hank

Colour B: #5102 Buttercream, 1 hank

NEEDLES

- 3.75 mm / US 5, set of 4 or 5 double-pointed needles or size needed to obtain correct tension

NOTIONS

- Stitch marker
- Locking stitch marker
- Stitch holders or waste yarn
- Tapestry needle

TENSION

22 sts and 42 rnds = 10 cm / 4 in. in Seed st

Be sure to check your tension.

Continued on page 140

NOTES

- These mitts are worked from the cuff up, primarily in seed stitch, with centred double increases along one edge for the thumb gusset. Each of the fingers and thumb is slightly longer than normal mittens, so the tapered claws do not squish fingertips nor become distorted by them.

- A locking stitch marker is placed at the centre of the thumb gusset so as not to interfere with the centred increases. Move the marker up as you work.

PATTERN STITCH

Seed Stitch (odd number of sts)
Rnd 1: K1, *p1, k1; rep from * to end of rnd.
Rnd 2: P1, *k1, p1; rep from * to end of rnd.
Rep Rnds 1 and 2 for patt.

MITTS
CUFF

With dpn and colour A, CO 23 (27, 29, 33, 35, 39) sts. Divide sts as evenly as possible over 3 or 4 needles. Pm and join to work in the rnd, being careful not to twist sts.

Work in Seed st for 11 (13, 14, 16, 17, 19) rnds.

Place locking marker in centre st of rnd for thumb gusset, with 11 (13, 14, 16, 17, 19) sts on each side of marked st.

THUMB GUSSET

Inc rnd: Work in established patt to marked st, (k1, yo, k1) in marked centre st, then work in patt to end of rnd – 2 sts inc'd.

Work 2 rnds even, working yo tbl to close hole.

Rep last 3 rnds 3 (4, 5, 6, 6, 7) more times –31 (37, 41, 47, 49, 55) sts.

DIVIDE HAND AND THUMB

Next rnd: Work 11 (13, 14, 16, 17, 19) sts in established patt, place 9 (11, 13, 15, 15, 17) gusset sts on holder or waste yarn for thumb, CO 1 st using Backward Loop method over gap, then work to end of rnd –23 (27, 29, 33, 35, 39) sts rem.

Cont even in established patt for 7 (10, 13, 15, 17, 18) rnds.

LITTLE FINGER

Next rnd: Work 5 (6, 7, 8, 8, 9) sts in established patt, place next 13 (15, 15, 17, 19, 21) sts on holder or waste yarn for big finger, CO 1 st using Backward Loop method over gap, then work to end of rnd –11 (13, 15, 17, 17, 19) sts rem.

Work 5 (6, 7, 8, 10, 10) rnds even.

Purl 1 rnd.

Cut colour A. Join colour B.

Knit 1 rnd.

SHAPE TIP

Setup (dec) rnd: Knit and dec 2 (1, 0, 2, 2, 1) st(s) evenly spaced across rnd –9 (12, 15, 15, 15, 18) sts rem.

SIZES 1–2 YEARS (2–4 YEARS, 4–6 YEARS, 6–8 YEARS, 8–12 YEARS) ONLY

Dec rnd 1: *K2 (3, 3, 3, 4), k2tog; rep from * 2 more times – 9 (12, 12, 12, 15) sts rem.

Knit 1 rnd even.

BEHIND THE SCENES:

Yoda's final look as a puppet was inspired by makeup artist Stuart Freeborn. His voice came from legendary puppet master Frank Oz, who did both acting and puppeteering duties in *The Empire Strikes Back* and *Return of the Jedi,* as well as the voicework on *The Phantom Menace, Attack of the Clones, Revenge of the Sith* and *The Last Jedi.*

'LUMINOUS BEINGS ARE WE, NOT THIS CRUDE MATTER.'

—YODA, STAR WARS: EPISODE V THE EMPIRE STRIKES BACK

SIZES 2-4 YEARS (4-6 YEARS, 6-8 YEARS, 8-12 YEARS) ONLY

Dec rnd 2: *K2 (2, 2, 3), k2tog; rep from * 2 more times –9 (9, 9, 12) sts rem.

Knit 1 rnd even.

SIZE 8-12 YEARS ONLY

Dec rnd 3: *K2, k2tog; rep from * 2 more times – 9 sts rem.

ALL SIZES

Dec rnd 4: *K1, k2tog; rep from * 2 more times – 6 sts rem.

Dec rnd 5: *K2tog; rep from * 2 more times – 3 sts rem.

Cut colour B, leaving a long tail. Thread tail through rem sts and pull tight to close hole. Secure on WS.

BIG FINGER

Return held 13 (15, 15, 17, 19, 21) sts for big finger to 2 dpn.

With third dpn and colour A, and with RS facing, pick up and knit 2 sts in CO edge, then work in established patt to end of rnd –15 (17, 17, 19, 21, 23) sts.

Divide sts evenly over 3 dpn. Pm and join to work in the rnd.

Work 5 (8, 11, 12, 13, 14) rnds even.

Purl 1 rnd.

Cut colour A. Join colour B.

Knit 1 rnd.

SHAPE TIP

Setup (dec) rnd: Knit and dec 0 (2, 2, 1, 0, 2) st(s) evenly spaced across rnd – 15 (15, 15, 18, 21, 21) sts rem.

Dec rnd 1: *K3 (3, 3, 4, 5, 5), k2tog; rep from * 2 more times – 12 (12, 12, 15, 18, 18) sts rem.

Knit 1 rnd even.

Dec rnd 2: *K2 (2, 2, 3, 4, 4), k2tog; rep from * 2 more times – 9 (9, 9, 12, 15, 15) sts rem.

Knit 1 rnd even.

SIZES 4-6 YEARS (6-8 YEARS, 8-12 YEARS) ONLY

Dec rnd 3: *K2 (3, 3), k2tog; rep from * 2 more times – 9 (12, 12) sts rem.

Knit 1 rnd even.

SIZES 6-8 YEARS (8-12 YEARS) ONLY

Dec rnd 4: *K2 (2), k2tog; rep from * 2 more times – 9 (9) sts rem.

Knit 1 rnd even.

ALL SIZES

Dec rnd 5: *K1, k2tog; rep from * 2 more times – 6 sts rem.

Dec rnd 6: *K2tog; rep from * 2 more times – 3 sts rem.

Cut colour B, leaving a long tail. Thread tail through rem sts and pull tight to close hole. Secure on WS.

THUMB

Return held 9 (11, 13, 15, 15, 17) sts for thumb to 2 dpn.

With third dpn and colour A, and with RS facing, pick up and knit 2 sts in CO edge, then work in established patt to end of rnd – 11 (13, 15, 17, 17, 19) sts.

Divide sts evenly over 3 dpn. Pm and join to work in the rnd.

Work 5 (6, 7, 8, 10, 10) rnds even.

Purl 1 rnd.

Cut colour A. Join colour B.

Knit 1 rnd.

SHAPE TIP

Setup (dec) rnd: Knit and dec 2 (1, 0, 2, 2, 1) st(s) evenly spaced across rnd – 9 (12, 15, 15, 15, 18) sts rem.

SIZES 1-2 YEARS (2-4 YEARS, 4-6 YEARS, 6-8 YEARS, 8-12 YEARS) ONLY

Dec rnd 1: *K2 (3, 3, 3, 4), k2tog; rep from * 2 more times – 9 (12, 12, 12, 15) sts rem.

Knit 1 rnd even.

SIZES 2-4 YEARS (4-6 YEARS, 6-8 YEARS, 8-12 YEARS) ONLY

Dec rnd 2: *K2 (2, 2, 3), k2tog; rep from * 2 more times – 9 (9, 9, 12) sts rem.

Knit 1 rnd even.

SIZE 8-12 YEARS ONLY

Dec rnd 3: *K2, k2tog; rep from * 2 more times – 9 sts rem.

Knit 1 rnd even.

ALL SIZES

Dec rnd 4: *K1, k2tog; rep from * 2 more times – 6 sts rem.

Dec rnd 5: *K2tog; rep from * 2 more times – 3 sts rem.

Cut colour B, leaving a long tail. Thread tail through rem sts and pull tight to close hole. Secure on WS.

FINISHING

Weave in ends. Block to measurements.

THE REBEL ALLIANCE SHAWL

Designed by: **SUSANNA IC**

LEVEL: ////

The symbol of the Rebel Alliance brings hope to many suffering under the oppression of the evil Empire and, later, under the First Order. The Rebel Alliance crest is reminiscent of a phoenix: a three-pronged arm extending off an arch. Called a *starbird*, it is often seen on Rebel pilot helmets and on a ring worn by mechanic Rose Tico in *The Last Jedi*.

This exquisite lace shawl is worked flat from the top down in one piece. Wrap and turn short row shaping is worked on a stocking-stitch background at the same time as the beaded Alliance crest, then the pattern gently flows into the delicate beaded lace section. Beading as you go with a small crochet hook means you can add as many or as few beads as you desire.

SIZE
One size

FINISHED MEASUREMENTS
Width: 216 cm / 85 in., blocked
Length at centre: 94 cm / 37 in., blocked

YARN
Colour A: Lace weight (lace #0) yarn, shown in Freia Fine Handpaints *Merino Lace Semi-Solid* (100% cruelty-free US merino wool; 434 m / 475 yd per 50 g / 1¾ oz cake) in colour Ecru, 1 cake

Colour B: Lace weight (lace #0) yarn, shown in Freia Fine Handpaints *Merino Lace Ombré Gradient* (100% cruelty-free US merino wool; 651 m / 712 yd per 75 g / 2.64 oz cake), in colour Sandbar, 2 cakes

NEEDLES
- 3.75 mm / US 5, 80 cm / 32 in. long circular needle or size needed to obtain correct tension
- 4.5 mm / US 7, 80 cm / 32 in. long circular needle
- 5 mm / US 8, 80 cm / 32 in. long circular needle
- 5.5 mm / US 9 needle for cast off

NOTIONS
- 1,800 seed beads, 4 mm / size 6/0
- 0.75 mm / US size 14/10 crochet hook
- Stitch markers (two different colours or types)
- Tapestry needle

TENSION
26 sts and 34 rows = 10 cm / 4 in. in St st with smallest needles, unblocked
Tension is not critical for this pattern, but the yarn weight and needle size used will affect the finished measurements.

Continued on page 146

NOTES

- Shawl is worked from the top down in one piece with short row shaping; it is worked flat, and circular needles are used to accommodate the large number of stitches.
- A firm cast on is important for the crescent, because the shape needs to be supported during blocking to allow the lace points to fully stretch; use a smaller needle if your cast on feels loose.
- One type (or colour) of stitch marker is used for the central placement of the Sigil Chart, and two different markers are used for short rows; make sure not to confuse them with the Sigil markers.
- The lace chart shows right-side rows only; work all wrong-side rows as follows: K1, k1-tbl, purl to last 2 sts, k1-tbl, k1.

SPECIAL TECHNIQUE

Place Bead (PB)

The beads are placed using a slender steel crochet hook. To place a bead on a stitch, insert the hook through the hole in the bead and slide the bead up onto the hook. Use the crochet hook to pick the stitch off the needle, then slide the bead down onto the stitch. Place the stitch back on the left needle, then knit it on RS rows or purl it on WS rows.

PATTERN STITCH

Stocking Stitch in Pattern (any number of sts)

Row 1 (RS): K2tog, yo, knit to last 2 sts, yo, ssk.
Row 2 (WS): K1, k1-tbl, purl to last 2 sts, k1-tbl, k1.
Rep Rows 1–2 for patt.

SHAWL

With colour A and smallest cir needle, CO 205 sts. Do not join.
Row 1 (RS): *K1-tbl; rep from * to end of row.
Rows 2–5: Knit.
Row 6 (WS): Purl.
Row 7 (RS): K4, PB, *k3, PB; rep from * to last 4 sts, k4.
Work 3 rows of St st in patt, ending with a WS row.
Inc row 1: K9, *(k1, yo, k1) in next st, k5; rep from * to last 10 sts, (k1, yo, k1) in next st, k9 – 269 sts.
Work 11 rows even in St st in patt, ending with a WS row.
Inc row 2: K4, [(k1, yo, k1) in next st, k5] 7 times, (k1, yo, k1) in next st, knit to last 47 sts, (k1, yo, k1) in next st, [k5, (k1, yo, k1) in next st] 7 times, k4 – 301 sts.
Work 1 row even.
Setup row (RS): K2tog, yo, k123, pm for Sigil patt, k51, pm for Sigil patt, k123, yo, ssk.
Work 1 row even.

SHORT ROWS

Short Row 1 (RS, setup): K2tog, yo, k1, pm for short row, knit to last 3 sts, w&t.
Short Row 2 (WS): P3, pm for short row, purl to next short row marker, remove marker, w&t.
Short Row 3: K3, pm for short row, knit to next short row marker, remove marker, w&t.
Rep Short Rows 2 and 3. *At the same time,* when 21 short rows have been worked, begin placing beads between Sigil markers every row, following Sigil Chart.
When chart is complete, remove Sigil markers and cont working rem short rows until fewer than 9 sts rem in work between short row markers on last RS short row, but do not w&t. Work to end of row in established St st in patt hiding wraps as you go, remove marker, yo, ssk.

Double check the number of sts to make sure you still have 301 sts; if needed, increase or decrease to the correct number on the next row.
Next row (WS): K1, k1-tbl, purl to last 2 sts hiding wraps as you go, remove marker, k1-tbl, k1.
Work 2 rows even in St st in patt, ending with a WS row.
Change to next larger cir needle and work 2 rows even, ending with a WS row.
Cut colour A and join colour B. Work 2 rows even, ending with a WS row.

BEGIN LACE CHART

Row 1 (inc, RS): K2tog, yo, k1, *k3, yo, k1, yo, k4; rep from * to last 2 sts, yo, ssk – 375 sts.
Row 2 and all other WS rows: K1, k1-tbl, purl to last 2 sts, k1-tbl, k1.
Work Rows 3–97 of Lace Chart – 597 sts. *Note: Each chart increase row adds 74 stitches.*
Change to next larger cir needle.
Work Rows 98–105 of Lace Chart – 671 sts.
Row 106 (WS): K11, p1, k8, *k9, p1, k8; rep from * to last 3 sts, k3.
Row 107 (RS): K11, PB, k9, *k8, PB, k9; rep from * to last 2 sts, k2.
Cast off with largest needle as follows: *K2tog, k1, return these 2 sts to LH needle; rep from * until 2 sts rem, return sts to LH needle, k2tog. Fasten off rem st.

FINISHING

Weave in ends, but don't trim the tails.
Wet block as shown in schematic, starting with the two short sides followed by the lace centre point, then pin out the rest of the points along the bottom edge (no pins are required along the top cast-on edge). Allow to dry completely.
Trim tails.

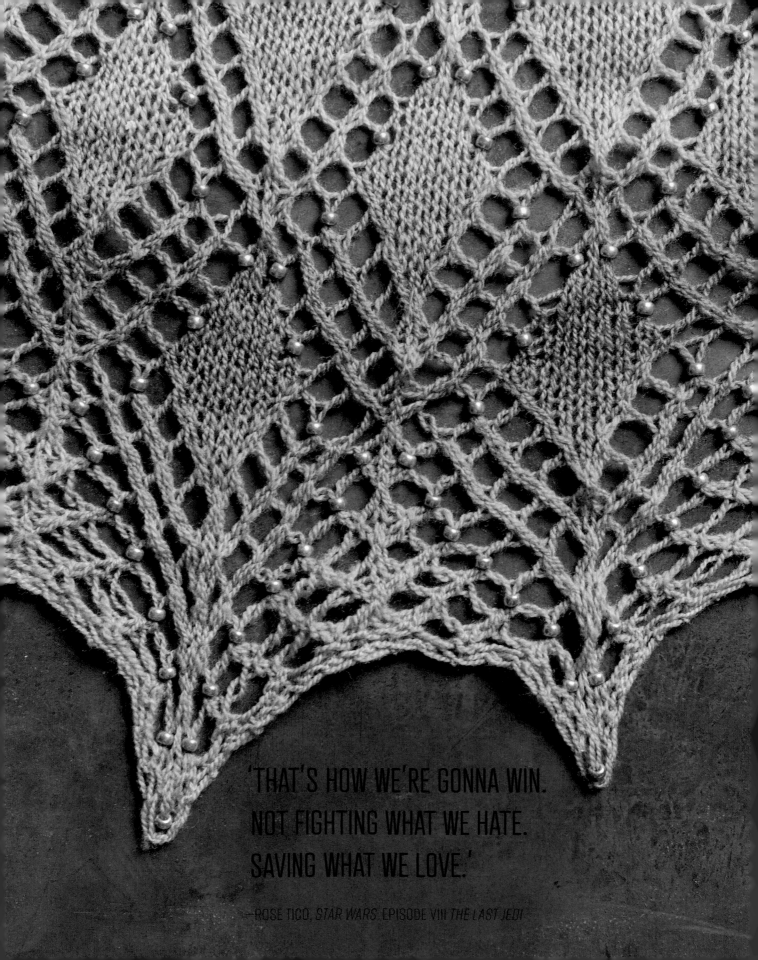

'THAT'S HOW WE'RE GONNA WIN.
NOT FIGHTING WHAT WE HATE.
SAVING WHAT WE LOVE.'

—ROSE TICO, *STAR WARS: EPISODE VIII THE LAST JEDI*

LACE CHART

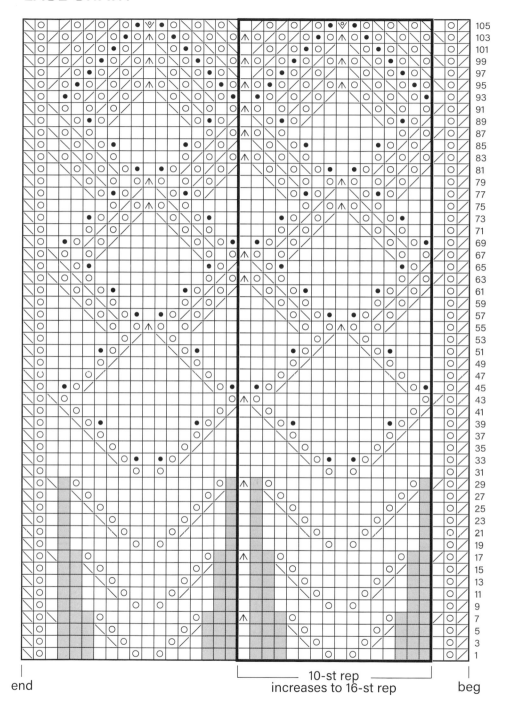

KEY

- ☐ knit
- ⊙ yo
- ● place bead
- ◢ k2tog
- ◣ ssk
- ⋏ s2kp
- ⋎ (k1, yo, k1) in same st
- ▨ no stitch
- ☐ repeat

end

10-st rep
increases to 16-st rep

beg

NOTE: Chart shows only odd-numbered rows.
Work all even-numbered rows: k1, k1-tbl, purl to last 2 sts, k1-tbl, k1.
Chart ends with Row 105.

SIGIL CHART

KEY

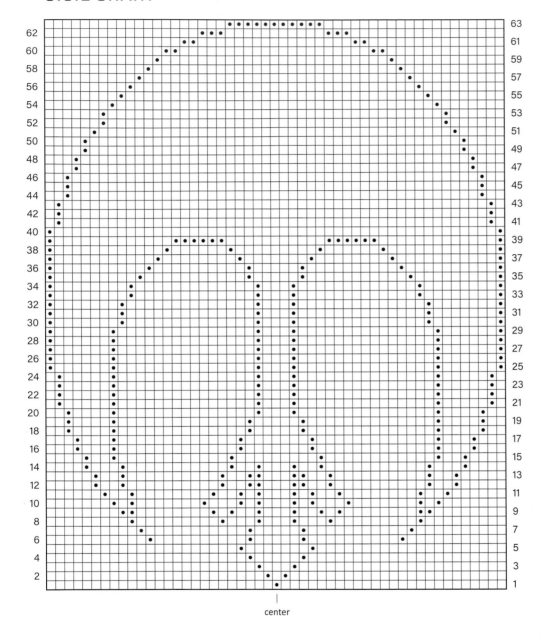

☐ k on RS, p on WS

⦿ place bead

center

Rose Tico wears a ring with a secret starbird crest insignia hidden inside. It was a way to silently show support to fellow rebels and was given to her by the Cobalt Squadron's commander to honour her sister, Paige, who died in battle.

216 cm / 85"

57 cm / 22½"

106.5 cm / 42"

94 cm
37"

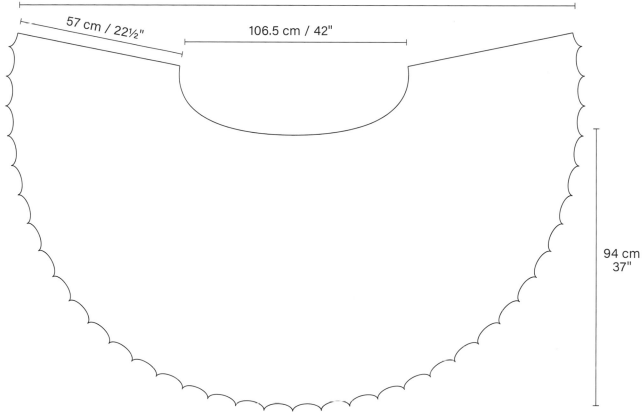

R2-D2 MITTENS

Designed by: **THERESE SHARP**

LEVEL: ////

One of the most popular droids in the *Star Wars* galaxy, R2-D2 is a common astromech droid – a brave and independent character who, as a result of his classification, is often unnoticed and underestimated by foes. Shaped like a small domed cylinder on moving hydraulic arm shafts and equipped with a language of beeps and whistles, Artoo is a veritable pocketknife with a myriad of tools and surprises hidden in his compartments. He can even fly! A key member of the Rebellion, often paired with his counterpart C-3PO, this plucky droid plays an important role in nearly every Saga film.

Knit from the bottom up in the round, these Fair Isle mittens start with a cable cast on and a simple 1x1 ribbed cuff. Stranded colourwork creates an R2-D2 on the hand side, while a secret message from the droid is worked across the palm. After the traditional mitten shaping is complete, the remaining stitches are gathered on a yarn tail, then an afterthought plain-coloured thumb is worked.

SIZE
One size

FINISHED MEASUREMENTS
Hand Circumference: 21.5 cm / 8½ in.
Length: 35 cm / 13¾ in.

YARN
3-ply weight (super fine #1) yarn, shown in Brooklyn Tweed *Peerie* (100% USA-grown merino wool; 192 m / 210 yd per 50 g / 1¾ oz hank)
Colour A: Admiral, 2 hanks
Colour B: Thaw, 1 hank
Colour C: Kettle, 1 hank
Colour D: Firebrush, 1 hank

NEEDLES
- 2 mm / US 0, 80 cm / 32 in. long circular needle, or set of 4 or 5 double-pointed needles
- 3 mm / US 2½, 80 cm / 32 in. long circular needle, or set of 4 or 5 double-pointed needles or size needed to obtain correct tension

NOTIONS
- Stitch markers
- Stitch holder or waste yarn
- Tapestry needle

TENSION
39 sts and 35 rnds = 10 cm / 4 in. in chart patt with larger needles
Be sure to check your tension.

Continued on page 154

- These mittens can be worked using one long circular needle using the Magic Loop method, or on a set of four or five double-pointed needles.
- Most knitters will knit the stranded colourwork section more tightly than plain stocking stitch. It's very important, especially when knitting small circumference pieces such as mittens, to maintain the tension and make sure the work retains its stretch.
- To avoid a stiff fabric, weave in floats every few stitches rather than every other stitch.

PATTERN STITCHES

Stocking Stitch (any number of sts)
Worked in the round, knit every rnd.

K1, P1 Rib (multiple of 2 sts)
All rnds: *K1, p1; rep from * to end of rnd.

MITTENS
CUFF

With smaller needles and colour A, CO 72 sts. Pm and join to work in the rnd, being careful not to twist sts.
Work in K1, P1 Rib for 5 cm / 2 in.
Inc rnd: *K5, k1f&b; rep from * to end of rnd – 84 sts.

HAND

Change to larger needles.
Work Rnds 1–44 of chart, joining colours B, C and D as indicated.

THUMB HOLE
LEFT MITTEN ONLY

Next rnd: Working Rnd 45 of chart, work in established patt to last 17 sts, place last 17 sts on holder or waste yarn, then CO 17 sts using Backward Loop method over opening, alternating colours in patt.

RIGHT MITTEN ONLY

Next rnd: Working Rnd 45 of chart, work 43 sts in established patt, place next 17 sts on holder or waste yarn, CO 17 sts using Backward Loop method over opening, alternating colours in patt, then work to end of rnd.

BOTH MITTENS

Work through Rnd 84 of chart. Pm after 42 sts.

SHAPE TOP

Dec rnd: Working next rnd of chart, k1, ssk, knit to 2 sts before marker, k2tog, sm, k1, ssk, work to last 2 sts, k2tog – 4 sts dec'd.
Rep last rnd 18 more times – 8 sts rem.
Cut yarn, leaving a long tail. Thread tail through rem sts and pull tight to close hole. Secure on WS.

THUMB

With smaller needles and RS facing, return 17 held sts to needle. With MC, pick up and knit 1 st in gap at side of thumb hole, 17 sts along CO edge, then 1 st in gap at side of thumb hole – 36 sts. Distribute sts evenly over needles with last st picked up at beg of rnd. Pm and join to work in the rnd.
Setup (dec) rnd: *Ssk, k16; rep from * once more – 34 sts rem.
Cont even in St st until thumb measures approx 7.5 cm / 3 in. or 2 cm / ¾ in. short of desired length. Pm after 17 sts.

SHAPE TOP

Dec rnd: *Ssk, knit to 2 sts before marker, k2tog; rep from * once more – 4 sts dec'd.
Rep dec rnd every rnd 6 more times – 6 sts rem.
Cut yarn, leaving a long tail. Thread tail through rem sts and pull tight to close hole. Secure on WS. Using duplicate st, add D to back of hands according to charts.

FINISHING

Weave in ends. Block to measurements.

BEHIND
THE SCENES:

In the original trilogy, R2-D2 was both a remote-controlled model that wheeled around on three legs and a rig worn by actor Kenny Baker.

CHART

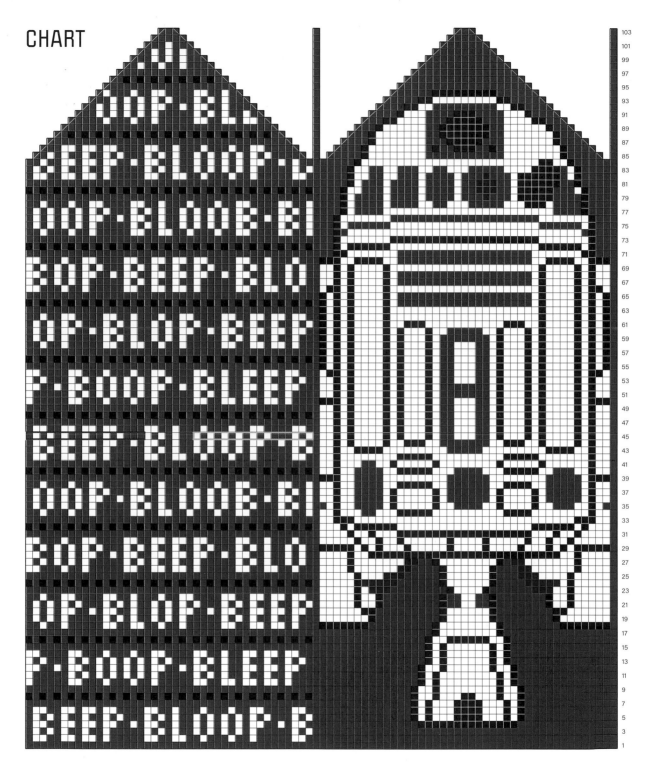

KEY

- ■ A
- □ B
- ■ C
- ■ work with C, duplicate st with D
- ◩ k2tog
- ◪ ssk
- □ right mitten thumb hole
- ■ left mitten thumb hole

WOOKIEE SOCKS

Designed by: **NATALIE SHELDON**

LEVEL: ////

An honourable and sophisticated people, Wookiees are known for their loyalty, intelligence and remarkable strength (they have been known to pull people's arms from their sockets when provoked). Hailing from the planet Kashyyyk, Wookiees were loyal to the Republic and fought to defend their planet from the Separatists in *Revenge of the Sith*. After many Jedi are slaughtered when Darth Sidious issues Order 66, Wookiee warrior Chewbacca and Chieftain Tarfful help Yoda escape in a hidden pod – an act that allows the Jedi Master to survive to eventually train a new apprentice: a young Luke Skywalker.

Knit from the top down in the round starting with a 2x2 rib, these Fair Isle socks feature a parade of Wookiees down the leg. The stranded colourwork sections are knit with a larger needle than the heel, toe and cuff, allowing for more stretch. An afterthought heel is added after the main portion of the sock is complete.

SIZE
One size

FINISHED MEASUREMENTS
Foot Circumference: 19 cm / 7½ in.
Leg Length: 24 cm / 9½ in.,
   including heel

YARN
3-ply weight (super fine #1) yarn,
   shown in Urban Girl Yarns *Virginia*
   (90% superwash merino, 10% nylon;
   439 m / 480 yd per 125 g / 4.4 oz
   hank)
Main Colour (MC): Tawny, 1 hank
Contrast Colour (CC): Kava, 1 hank

NEEDLES
- 2.25 mm / US 1, set of 4 double-
  pointed needles
- 2.75 mm / US 2, 23 cm / 9 in. long
  circular needle or size needed to
  obtain correct tension

NOTIONS
- Stitch markers
- Waste yarn
- Tapestry needle

TENSION
38½ sts and 39 rnds = 10 cm / 4 in. in
   chart patt with larger needles
Be sure to check your tension.

NOTES
- These socks are knit in the round
  from the top down using stranded
  colourwork.

Continued on page 160

- Although double-pointed needles and a short circular needle are used for making these socks, you may also use one long circular needle and work using the Magic Loop method, or two short circular needles. If you're working with either one of these alternative methods, the stitches for Needle 1 should be on the first half of a long circular needle, or one of the short circular needles, and the stitches for Needles 2 and 3 should be on the second half of the long circular needle, or on the second short circular needle.
- An afterthought heel is knit after the main portion of the sock is complete. Using waste yarn with a high contrast to the working yarn colours will aid in the placement of the heel.

PATTERN STITCHES

K2, P2 Rib (multiple of 4 sts)

All rnds: *K2, p2; rep from * to end of rnd.

Stocking Stitch (any number of sts)

Worked in the round, knit every rnd.

SOCKS

CUFF

With smaller needles and CC, CO 72 sts using Long Tail method. Pm and join to work in the rnd, being careful not to twist sts.

Work in K2, P2 Rib for approx 4 cm / 1½ in.

Knit 1 rnd.

Join MC and knit 1 rnd.

LEG

Change to larger needles.

Beg Chart A, working Rnds 1–53 and working 36-st rep twice across rnd.

Cut CC, leaving a long tail.

HEEL PLACEMENT

Turn work with WS facing, p36 with waste yarn, turn. Cut waste yarn and join CC. With RS facing, knit 36 sts just worked with waste yarn; this becomes the first row of the heel, and rnds now beg with top of foot.

FOOT

Work Rnds 1–54 of Chart B.

Knit 1 rnd with MC. Cut MC, leaving a long tail.

Foot should measure approx 14 cm / 5½ in. from waste yarn at heel. If necessary cont even with CC until foot measures 9 cm / 3½ in. short of desired length of foot.

TOE

Change to smaller needles. Arrange sts with 36 sts on Needle 1 for the top of the foot and 18 sts each on Needles 2 and 3 for the sole.

Next rnd: Working with CC only, knit.

Dec rnd: Needle 1, k1, ssk, knit to last 3 sts on needle, k2tog, k1; Needle 2, k1, ssk, knit to end of needle; Needle 3, knit to last 3 sts, k2tog, k1 – 4 sts dec'd.

Rep last 2 rnds 11 more times – 24 sts rem.

Slip sts from Needle 3 to Needle 2. Join rem sts using Kitchener st.

HEEL

With smaller needles, place 36 sts directly above waste yarn onto Needle 1, then divide the rem 36 sts below the waste yarn evenly between Needles 2 and 3, with 18 sts on each needle – 72 total. Carefully remove waste yarn.

Pm and join to work in the rnd, beg rnds with Needle 1.

Join CC.

'GO, I WILL. GOOD RELATIONS WITH THE WOOKIEES, I HAVE.'

—YODA, STAR WARS: EPISODE III REVENGE OF THE SITH

Next rnd: Knit.

Dec rnd: Needle 1, k1, ssk, knit to last 3 sts on needle, k2tog, k1; Needle 2, k1, ssk, knit to end of needle; Needle 3, knit to last 3 sts, k2tog, k1 – 4 sts dec'd.

Rep last 2 rnds 11 more times – 24 sts rem.

Slip sts from Needle 3 to Needle 2. Join rem sts using Kitchener st.

FINISHING

Weave in ends, using tails at heel to close any gaps at each corner. Block.

CHART A

36-st rep
work twice across each rnd

KEY

☐ MC

■ CC

☐ repeat

CHART B

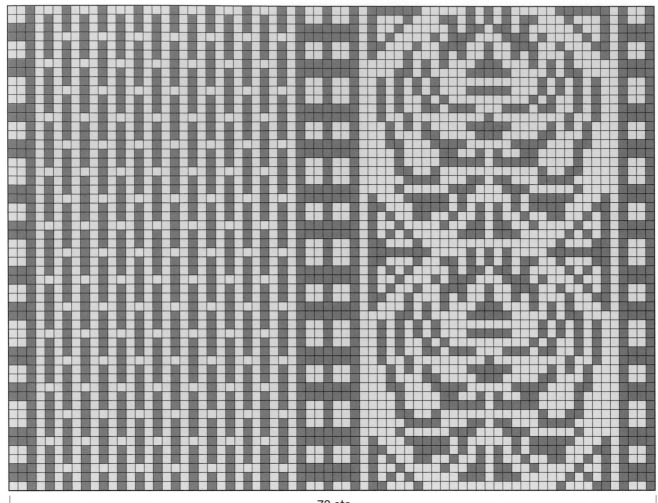

─72 sts─
work once across each rnd

KEY

☐ MC

■ CC

☐ repeat

DARTH VADER PULLOVER

Designed by: **STEPHANIE LOTVEN**

LEVEL: ////

One of the most famous movie villains of all time, Darth Vader is known for his striking costume, epic orchestral theme and deep, authoritative voice. In the prequel trilogy, we learn the details of Vader's youth as Anakin Skywalker, a powerful Jedi who is ultimately seduced to the dark side by Darth Sidious. Left for dead by Obi-Wan Kenobi on the volcanic planet of Mustafar in *Revenge of the Sith*, Anakin is taken to Coruscant, where his mangled body is replaced with machine parts. Imprisoned inside a helmet and black armour with a central control panel on the torso keeping him on life support, Vader emerges as the brutal enforcer for the Empire and all-around bad guy audiences know and love.

Now you can channel Vader's power with this magnificent pullover inspired by his armour's control panel. Knit in the round from the top down, the yoke is knit in a traditional stranded colourwork technique. After dividing the body and sleeves, the torso is worked in a plain colour to the bottom hem, then the sleeves are picked up and knit in stocking stitch in the round to the cuffs. The utility belt and control panel are duplicate stitched onto the front for a maximum evil effect.

SIZES

XS (S, M, L, XL, 2XL, 3XL, 4XL)
Shown in size S.
Instructions are written for the smallest size, with larger sizes given in brackets; when only one number is given, it applies to all sizes.

FINISHED MEASUREMENTS

Chest: 86.5 (96, 105.5, 115, 124.5, 134, 143.5, 153) cm / 34 (37¾, 41½, 45¼, 49, 52¾, 56½, 60¼) in.

Length at centre front: 56 (56, 58.5, 59.5, 62, 63.5, 66, 67.5) cm / 22 (22, 23, 23½, 24½, 25, 26, 26½) in.

YARN

Aran weight (medium #4) yarn, shown in LolaBean Yarn Co. *Kidney Bean* (100% superwash merino; 200 m / 218 yd per 100 g / 3½ oz hank)

Main Colour (MC): Darkness Falls, 5 (5, 6, 6, 7, 7, 8, 9) hanks

Contrasting Colour 1 (CC1): Chromatic, 1 (1, 1, 2, 2, 2, 2, 2) hank(s)

Contrasting Colour 2 (CC2): Paint the Town Red, 1 hank

Contrasting Colour 3 (CC3): Out of the Blue, 1 hank

NEEDLES

- 4.5 mm / US 7, 40 cm / 16 in. and 80 cm / 32 in. long circular needles and set of 4 or 5 double-pointed needles
- 5.5 mm / US 9, 40 cm / 16 in. and 80 cm / 32 in. long circular needles and set of 4 or 5 double-pointed needles or size needed to obtain correct tension

Continued on page 166

YOKE

With shorter smaller cir needle and
    MC, CO 72 (76, 78, 80, 84, 88, 94, 94)
    sts. Pm and join to work in the rnd,
    being careful not to twist sts. *Rnds
    beg at centre back of neck.*
Work in K1, P1 Rib for 2 cm / ¾ in.
Change to shorter larger cir needle,
    then change to longer larger cir
    needle when there are too many
    sts to work comfortably on shorter
    needle.
Knit 1 rnd even.

SIZES XS (S, M, L, XL) ONLY

Inc Rnd 1: *K4 (4, 2, 2, 2), M1L; rep
    from * to end of rnd – 90 (95, 117,
    120, 126) sts.
Knit 1 rnd even.

SIZES 2XL (4XL) ONLY

Inc Rnd 1: (K2, M1L) 35 (38) times, (k3,
    M1L) 6 times – 129 (138) sts.
Knit 1 rnd even.

SIZE 3XL ONLY

Inc Rnd 1: (K2, M1L, k3, M1L) 18 times,
    (k2, M1L) twice –132 sts.
Knit 1 rnd even.

SIZES XS (S, M, L, XL, 3XL, 4XL) ONLY

Inc Rnd 2: *K15 (7, 39, 15, 9, 8, 6), M1L;
    rep from * 5 (12, 2, 7, 13, 15, 21) more
    times, k0 (4, 0, 0, 0, 4, 6) –96 (108,
    120, 128, 140, 148, 160) sts.
Knit 1 rnd even.

SIZE 2XL ONLY

Inc Rnd 2: (K6, M1L, K5, M1L) 9 times,
    (k6, M1L) 5 times –152 sts.
Knit 1 rnd even.

ALL SIZES

SHAPE BACK NECK

Short Row 1 (RS): K28 (32, 36, 38, 42, 45,
    46, 48), w&t.
Short Row 2 (WS): Purl to beg-of-rnd
    marker, sm, p28 (32, 36, 38, 42, 45, 46,
    48), w&t.

'NO. I AM YOUR FATHER.'

—DARTH VADER, *STAR WARS*: EPISODE V *THE EMPIRE STRIKES BACK*

Short Row 3: Knit to 4 sts before wrapped st, w&t.

Short Row 4: Purl to 4 sts before wrapped st, w&t.

Short Row 5: Knit to beg-of-rnd marker. Do not turn.

Next rnd: Knit, picking up wraps as you come to them.

Next rnd: Remove beg-of-rnd marker, k72 (81, 90, 96, 105, 114, 111, 120), pm for new beg of rnd. *Rnds beg at centre of left shoulder.*

Join CC1.

Colourwork setup rnd: *K1 (2, 3, 2, 3, 4, 2, 3) MC, pm, k10 (10, 10, 12, 12, 12, 14, 14) CC1, pm, k1 (2, 3, 2, 3, 4, 2, 3) MC, pm, k8 (8, 8, 10, 10, 10, 12, 12) CC1, pm, k1 (2, 3, 2, 3, 4, 2, 3) MC, pm, k6 (6, 6, 8, 8, 8, 10, 10) CC1, pm, k1 (2, 3, 2, 3, 4, 2, 3) MC, pm, k8 (8, 8, 10, 10, 10, 12, 12) CC1, pm, k1 (2, 3, 2, 3, 4, 2, 3) MC, pm, k10 (10, 10, 12, 12, 12, 14, 14) CC1, pm, k1 (2, 3, 2, 3, 4, 2, 3) MC, pm; rep from * once more – 10 segments of MC and 10 segments of CC1.

When working the colour-stranded patt, knit all sts using the colours as established. All increases are worked with MC only and should be made by picking up the MC strand and knitting through the back loop with MC.

Rnd 1: Knit in established colours and sm as you come to them.

Rnd 2 (inc): *(Knit MC to marker, M1L MC, sm, knit CC1 to marker, sm) 5 times, M1R MC; rep from * once more, then knit to end of rnd – 12 sts inc'd.

Rnd 3: Work even.

Rnd 4 (inc): *Knit MC to marker, M1L MC, sm, (knit CC1 to marker, sm, M1R MC, knit MC to marker, sm) 4 times, knit CC1 to marker, sm, M1R MC; rep from * once more – 12 sts inc'd.

Rep last 4 rnds 3 (4, 4, 5, 5, 6, 7, 7) more times – 192 (228, 240, 272, 284, 320, 340, 352) sts.

Rep first 2 rnds 1 (0, 1, 0, 1, 0, 0, 1) more time – 204 (228, 252, 272, 296, 320, 340, 364) sts.

Work 11 (9, 9, 7, 7, 5, 3, 3) rnds even in patt.

Cut CC1, leaving a long tail.

Next rnd: With MC only, knit to end of rnd and remove all markers, then k51 (60, 63, 71, 74, 83, 88, 91), pm for new beg of rnd. *Rnds beg at centre of back; adjust beg-of-rnd marker placement if needed so rnds beg at centre of narrow CC1 band.*

SIZE XS ONLY

Knit 1 rnd even.

SIZES S (M, L, XL, 2XL, 3XL, 4XL) ONLY

Inc rnd: *K114 (63, 136, 74, 40, 56, 45), M1L; rep from * 1 (3, 1, 3, 7, 5, 7) more times, k0 (0, 0, 0, 0, 4, 4) – 230 (256, 274, 300, 328, 346, 372) sts.

ALL SIZES

Knit 2 rnds even.

SHAPE LOWER YOKE

Short Row 1 (RS): K61 (69, 77, 82, 90, 98, 104, 112), w&t.

Short Row 2 (WS): Purl to marker, sm, p61 (69, 77, 82, 90, 98, 104, 112), w&t.

Short Row 3: Knit to 4 sts before wrapped st, w&t.

Short Row 4: Purl to 4 sts before wrapped st, w&t.

Short Row 5: Knit to marker. Do not turn.

Next rnd: Knit, picking up wraps as you come to them.

Cont even in St st until piece measures approx 24 (24, 25.5, 26.5, 28, 29, 30.5, 32) cm / 9½ (9½, 10, 10½, 11, 11½, 12, 12½) in. from CO edge at back neck.

DIVIDE BODY AND SLEEVES

Next rnd: K32 (36, 40, 43, 47, 51, 54, 58) sts for right back, place next 38 (43, 48, 51, 56, 62, 65, 70) sts on holder or waste yarn for sleeve, CO 8 (8, 8, 10, 10, 10, 12, 12) sts using Backward Loop method, k64 (72, 80, 86, 94, 102, 108, 116) front sts, place next 38 (43, 48, 51, 56, 62, 65, 70) sts on holder or waste yarn, CO 8 (8, 8, 10, 10, 10, 12, 12) sts, then k32 (36, 40, 43, 47, 51, 54, 58) sts for left back – 144 (160, 176, 192, 208, 224, 240, 256) sts.

BODY

Work even in St st until body measures 32.5 (32.5, 33.5, 33.5, 35, 35, 36, 36) cm / 12¾ (12¾, 13¼, 13¼, 13¾, 13¾, 14¼, 14¼) in. from underarm CO.

Change to longer smaller cir needle.

Work in K1, P1 Rib for 3 cm / 1¼ in. Cast off loosely in patt.

BEHIND THE SCENES:

While it was British actor David Prowse inside the Darth Vader costume in most scenes, George Lucas wanted a more intimidating voice for his menacing villain. James Earl Jones was cast and his voiceover was added in postproduction.

SLEEVES

Place 38 (43, 48, 51, 56, 62, 65, 70) sleeve sts on larger dpn.

With MC, beg at centre of underarm CO, pick up and knit 4 (4, 4, 5, 5, 5, 6, 6) sts, knit sleeve sts, then pick up and knit 4 (4, 4, 5, 5, 5, 6, 6) sts along rem underarm CO. Pm and join to work in the rnd – 46 (51, 56, 61, 66, 72, 77, 82) sts.

Next rnd: Knit and dec 0 (1, 0, 1, 0, 0, 1, 0) st(s) at beg of rnd – 46 (50, 56, 60, 66, 72, 76, 82) sts.

Knit 15 (12, 11, 8, 7, 6, 6, 5) rnds even.

Dec rnd: K1, k2tog, knit to last 3 sts, ssk, k1 – 2 sts dec'd.

Rep Dec rnd every 16 (13, 12, 9, 8, 7, 7, 6) rnds 2 (3, 3, 9, 11, 7, 7, 8) more times, then every 15 (12, 11, 0, 0, 6, 6, 5) rnds

2 (3, 4, 0, 0, 7, 7, 9) times – 36 (36, 40, 40, 42, 42, 46, 46) sts rem.

Cont even until sleeve measures 37.5 (39.5, 40.5, 40.5, 42, 42, 43, 43) cm / 14¾ (15½, 16, 16, 16½, 16½, 17, 17) in. from underarm CO.

Change to smaller dpn.

Work in K1, P1 Rib for 5 cm / 2 in. Cast off loosely in patt.

FINISHING

Using duplicate st and appropriate colours, work Control Panel chart at centre of front and approx 3 cm / 1¼ in. below yoke colourwork patt. *Place removable marker at centre of narrow CC1 band on centre front as a guide to placement of chart patt.*

Work Utility Belt Chart A with duplicate st centred on front and approx 5.5 cm / 2¼ in. below Control Panel or at waist.

Work Utility Belt Chart B with duplicate st approx 2 cm / ¾ in. to left of Utility Belt Chart A as viewed from front (see photo for reference). Make sure top row of Chart B is even with top of Chart A.

Work Utility Belt Chart C with duplicate st approx 2 cm / ¾ in. to right of Utility Belt Chart A as viewed from front (see photo for reference). Make sure top row of Chart C is even with top of Chart A.

Weave in ends. Block to measurements.

NOTES

- These mittens can be worked using one long circular needle using the Magic Loop method, or a set of four or five double-pointed needles.
- Most knitters will knit stranded colourwork section more tightly than plain stocking stitch. It's very important, especially when knitting small circumference pieces such as mittens, to maintain the tension and make sure the work retains its stretch.
- If the floated colour is woven in every other stitch, this will use more yarn than weaving in every few stitches, and can create a stiff fabric.

PATTERN STITCHES

Stocking Stitch (any number of sts)
Worked in the round, knit every rnd.

K1, P1 Rib (multiple of 2 sts)
All rnds: *K1, p1; rep from * to end of rnd.

MITTENS

CUFF

With smaller needles and MC, CO 72 sts. Pm and join to work in the rnd, being careful not to twist sts.
Work in K1, P1 Rib for 5 cm / 2 in.
Inc rnd: *K5, k1f&b; rep from * to end of rnd – 84 sts.

HAND

Change to larger needles.
Join CC.
Work Rnds 1–39 of chart.

THUMB HOLE

LEFT MITTEN ONLY

Next rnd: Working Rnd 40 of chart, work in established patt to last 17 sts, place last 17 sts on holder or waste yarn, then CO 17 sts using Backward Loop method over opening, alternating colours in patt.

RIGHT MITTEN ONLY

Next rnd: Working Rnd 40 of chart, work 43 sts in established patt, place next 17 sts on holder or waste yarn, CO 17 sts using Backward Loop method over opening, alternating colours in patt, then work to end of rnd.

BOTH MITTENS

Cont through Rnd 80 of chart. Pm after 42 sts.

SHAPE TOP

Dec rnd: Working next rnd of chart, k1, ssk, knit to 2 sts before marker, k2tog, sm, k1, ssk, work to last 2 sts, k2tog –4 sts dec'd.
Rep last rnd 18 more times – 8 sts rem.
Cut yarn, leaving a long tail. Thread tail through rem sts and pull tight to close hole. Secure on WS.

THUMB

With smaller needles and RS facing, return 17 held sts to needle, with MC, pick up and knit 1 st in gap at side of thumb hole, 17 sts along CO edge, then 1 st in gap at side of thumb hole – 36 sts. Distribute sts evenly over needles with last st picked up at beg of rnd. Pm and join to work in the rnd.
Setup (dec) rnd: *Ssk, k16; rep from * once more – 34 sts rem.
Cont even in St st until thumb measures approx 7.5 cm / 3 in. or 2 cm / ¾ in. short of desired length. Pm after 17 sts.

SHAPE TOP

Dec rnd: *Ssk, knit to 2 sts before marker, k2tog; rep from * once more – 4 sts dec'd.
Rep dec rnd every rnd 6 more times – 6 sts rem.
Cut yarn, leaving a long tail. Thread tail through rem sts and pull tight to close hole. Secure on WS.

FINISHING

Weave in ends. Block to measurements.

'AT LAST WE WILL REVEAL OURSELVES TO THE JEDI. AT LAST WE WILL HAVE REVENGE.'

—DARTH MAUL, *STAR WARS*: EPISODE I *THE PHANTOM MENACE*

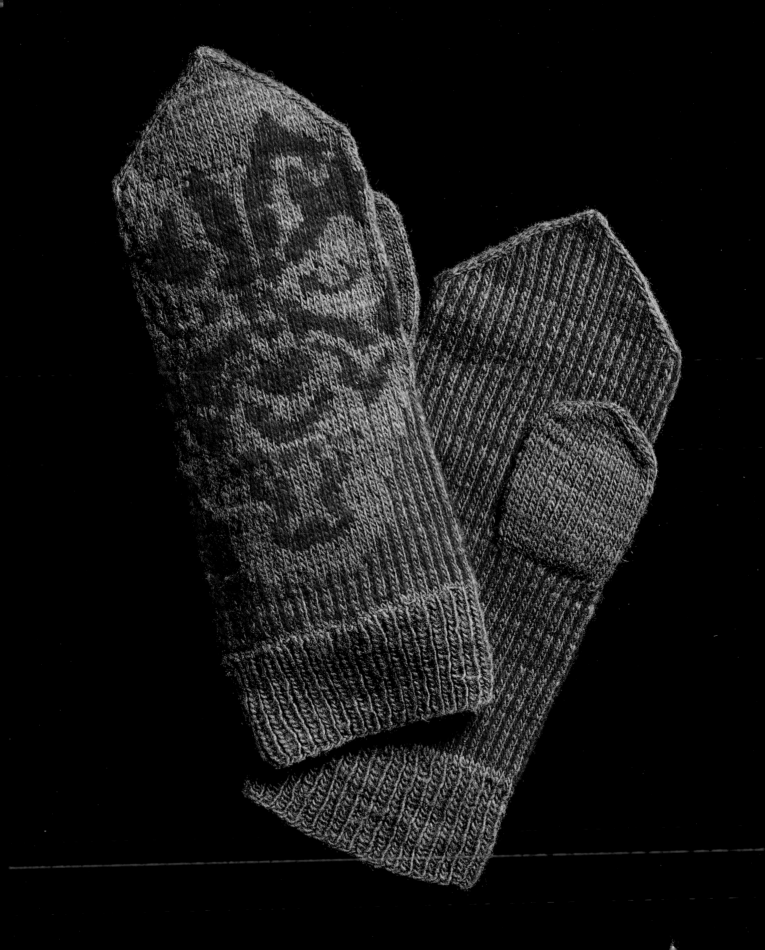

BEHIND THE SCENES: Darth Maul's double-bladed lightsaber was the first of its kind to be seen in a *Star Wars* film and had only previously been described or imagined in expanded universe content.

CHART

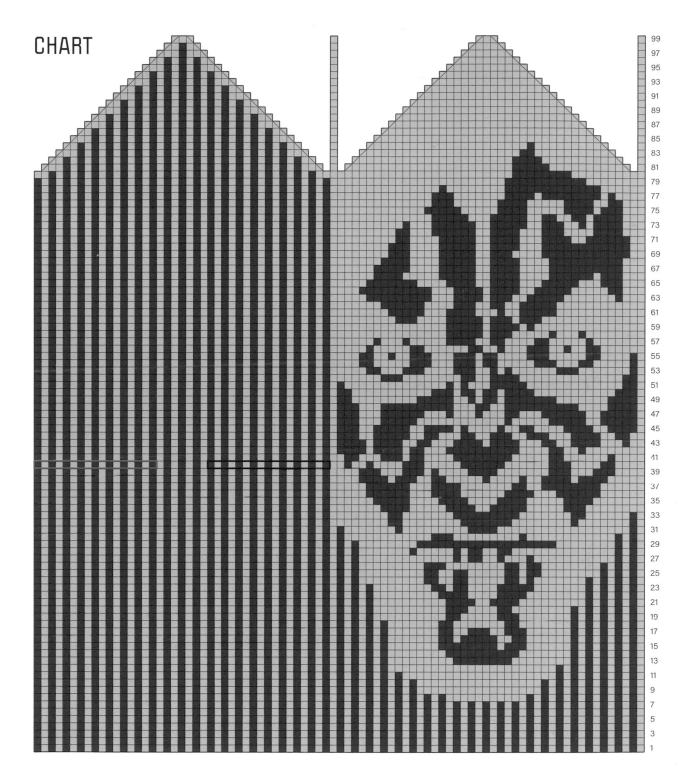

99
97
95
93
91
89
87
85
83
81
79
77
75
73
71
69
67
65
63
61
59
57
55
53
51
49
47
45
43
41
39
37
35
33
31
29
27
25
23
21
19
17
15
13
11
9
7
5
3
1

KEY

◻ MC   ◩ ssk
◼ CC   ▢ right mitten thumb hole
◩ k2tog   ▢ left mitten thumb hole

CLONE TROOPER HAT

Designed by: **TANIS GRAY**

LEVEL: ///

Created from the DNA of bounty hunter Jango Fett, the clone army was secretly commissioned by Count Dooku and Chancellor Palpatine under false pretences that it was necessary to protect the Republic from a potential future galactic war. Growing at an accelerated rate on the planet Kamino, the clone army numbered in the thousands and was trained to obey orders without hesitation. Nearly identical in appearance, most phase one clones wear a distinct white helmet and matching armour – a precursor to the stormtroopers to come.

Knit in the round from the bottom up, this bold unisex hat starts off with corrugated ribbing. High-contrast clone trooper helmets worked in stranded colourwork march across the body of the hat, just as they do in battle, while the crown decreases spiral upwards in the main colour. Attach a tassel or pom-pom to stand out from the other clones.

SIZES
S (L)
Shown in size S.
Instructions are written for the smaller size, with larger size given in brackets; when only one number is given, it applies to both sizes.

FINISHED MEASUREMENTS
Circumference: 49 (56) cm / 19¼ (22) in.
Length: 23 (24) cm / 9 (9½) in.

YARN
3-ply weight (super fine #1) yarn, shown in The Fiberists *Audubon Unum Fingering* (100% superwash merino wool; 397 m / 434 yd per 114 g / 4 oz hank)
Colour A: Graphite, 1 hank
Colour B: Diamond, 1 hank

NEEDLES
- 3.25 mm / US 3, 40 cm / 16 in. long circular needle and set of 4 or 5 double-pointed needles or size needed to obtain correct tension

NOTIONS
- Stitch markers
- Tapestry needle

TENSION
29 sts and 44 rnds = 10 cm / 4 in. in chart patt
Be sure to check your tension.

Continued on page 180

HAT

With cir needle and colour A, CO 132 (152) sts using twisted German method. Pm and join to work in the rnd, being careful not to twist sts.

Join colour B. Work in Corrugated Rib for 10 rnds.

Next rnd: Knit with colour A.

Inc rnd: With colour A, k17 (6), M1L, *k16 (20), M1L; rep from * to last 3 (6) sts, k3 (6) – 140 (160) sts.

Work Rnds 1–39 of Fair Isle chart. *Note:* It may help if you place a marker at the end of each repeat.

Cut colour B.

With colour A only, cont in St st until piece measures 18.5 (19.5) cm / 7¼ (7¾) in. from beg.

SHAPE CROWN

Change to dpn when there are too few sts to work comfortably on cir needle.

Dec rnd 1: *K18, k2tog, pm; rep from * to end of rnd – 133 (152) sts rem.

Dec rnds 2–18: *Knit to 2 sts before marker, k2tog; rep from * to end of rnd – 14 (16) sts rem.

Dec rnd 19: *K2tog; rep from * to end of rnd – 7 (8) sts rem.

Cut yarn, leaving a long tail. Thread tail through rem sts and pull tight to close hole. Secure on WS.

FINISHING

Weave in ends. Block to measurements.

CHART

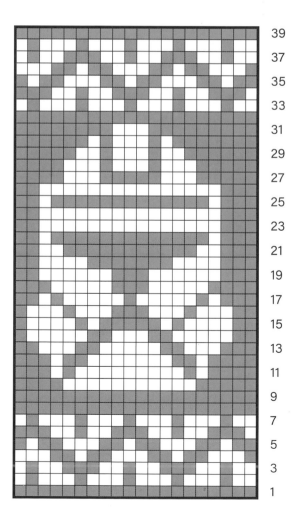

KEY

■ A
□ B
☐ repeat

39
37
35
33
31
29
27
25
23
21
19
17
15
13
11
9
7
5
3
1

HOME DECOR

'CHEWIE, WE'RE HOME.'

—HAN SOLO, *STAR WARS: EPISODE VII THE FORCE AWAKENS*

BB-8
THROW BLANKET

Designed by: **TANIS GRAY**

LEVEL: ✎

One of the breakout characters of *The Force Awakens*, BB-8 was a new kind of droid in the *Star Wars* saga. A ball-shaped astromech droid specialising in ship repair and navigation, his unique orange-and-white spherical shape lends itself to travelling at high speeds. His tool-bay discs allow him to hide an array of tools and weapons inside his body. Belonging to Resistance leader Poe Dameron, BB-8 is a fiercely loyal, brave and important member of the group, aiding them in many missions and delivering comic relief.

Using only the simple knit stitch, this blanket is worked in long vertical strips. Each strip is mattress stitched together, creating a pixelated version of everyone's favourite new droid. Size the blanket up or down by simply changing the yarn weight and needle size, and snuggle away.

SIZES
One size

FINISHED MEASUREMENTS
Width: 87 cm / 34¼ in.
Length: 118 cm / 46½ in.

YARN
Aran weight (medium #4) yarn, shown in Berroco *Comfort* (50% super fine acrylic, 50% super fine nylon; 193 m / 210 yd per 100 g / 3.5 oz skein)
Colour A: #9731 Kidz Orange, 4 skeins
Colour B: #9734 Liquorice, 4 skeins
Colour C: #9701 Ivory, 3 skeins
Colour D: #9770 Ash Grey, 1 skein

NEEDLES
- 5 mm / US 8 needles or size needed to obtain correct tension

NOTION
- Tapestry needle

TENSION
16 sts and 37 rows = 10 cm / 4 in. in Garter st
Each strip should measure approx 5 cm / 2 in. wide after seaming.
Be sure to check your tension.

Continued on page 186

- This blanket is worked in 17 separate garter-stitch strips, each from the bottom up. Each square on the chart represents 18 rows of garter stitch, or 9 ridges. Cut the yarn every time you change colours and do not carry yarn up the sides. Strips are joined using mattress stitch after all the strips are made.

PATTERN STITCH
Garter Stitch (any number of sts)
All rows: Knit.

BLANKET
STRIP 1

With A, CO 10 sts.
Working in Garter st, follow column 1 from block 1 through block 24 at top of chart – 432 rows total.
Cast off all sts pwise.

STRIPS 2–17

Working same as Strip 1, follow each of the other columns from block 1 to block 24. *Note:* It may make it easier to assemble the strips if you label each one as you complete it.

FINISHING

Sew strips tog in order as shown in chart using mattress st.
Weave in ends. Block to measurements.

BEHIND THE SCENES:

BB-8 stands at about 66 cm / 2' 2" tall and has tiny lights on his frame that on-set technicians could blink faster or slower depending on what emotion they wanted to convey.

'I NAMED HIM BB-8 BECAUSE IT WAS ALMOST ONOMATOPOEIA. IT WAS SORT OF HOW HE LOOKED TO ME, WITH THE 8, OBVIOUSLY, AND THEN THE TWO B'S.'

—J.J. ABRAMS, DIRECTOR OF *STAR WARS*: EPISODE VII *THE FORCE AWAKENS*

CHART

KEY

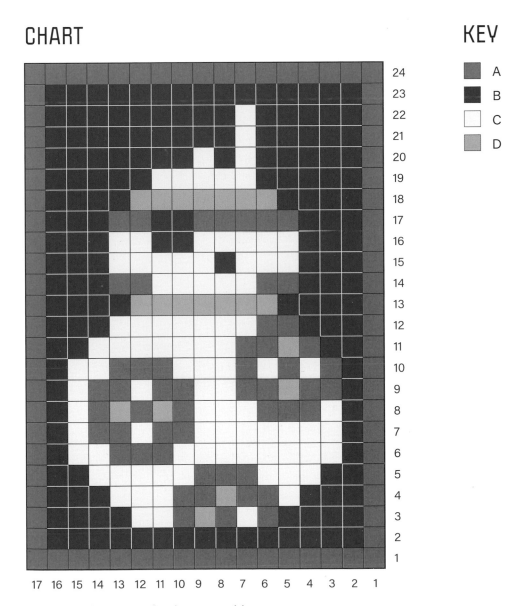

■ (A)	A
■ (B)	B
□ (C)	C
■ (D)	D

NOTE: each square equals 10 sts wide and 18 rows (9 ridges) high

DROID SCATTER CUSHION SET

Designed by: **TANIS GRAY**

LEVEL: ///

Star Wars has its fair share of iconic partnerships, but C-3PO and R2-D2 are unique in that their friendship extends across all nine Skywalker Saga films. Opposites in both appearance and personality – C-3PO is a tall, fussy worrywart who speaks over six million languages, while R2-D2 is short, easygoing and speaks only in binary – together they make up the perfect team. This pair of droid cushions features the faces of these two unforgettable characters, allowing *Star Wars* fans to keep the spirit of Artoo and Threepio in their very own homes.

Knit back and forth, worked flat and begun with a provisional cast on, the front panel is worked in a combination of stranded colourwork and duplicate stitch to make colour management easier. A purl turning ridge is worked, then the plain-coloured backing goes quickly in stocking stitch. A second purl turning ridge is executed, the cast on removed, then the live stitches are grafted together. Side seams are closed up with mattress stitch, enclosing a 40.5 x 40.5 cm / 16 x 16" cushion pad. Colourful and fun, this classic duo makes a great addition to any couch or bedroom.

SIZE
One size

FINISHED MEASUREMENTS
Width: 40.5 cm / 16 in.
Height: 40.5 cm / 16 in.

YARN
Aran weight (medium #4) yarn, shown in Kelbourne Woolens *Germantown* (100% North American wool; 201 m / 220 yd per 100 g / 3½ oz skein)

R2-D2:
Main Colour (MC): #419 Oxford Blue, 2 skeins
Contrast Colour 1 (CC1): #105 Natural, 1 skein
Contrast Colour 2 (CC2): #625 Scarlet, 1 skein
Contrast Colour 3 (CC3): #005 Black, 1 skein
Contrast Colour 4 (CC4): #059 Pebble, 1 skein

C-3PO:
Main Colour (MC): #725 Goldenrod, 2 skeins
Contrast Colour 1 (CC1): #708 Honey, 1 skein

NEEDLES
- 5 mm / US 8, 60 cm / 24 in. long circular needle or size needed to obtain correct tension

NOTIONS
- Waste yarn
- 4 mm / US G-6 crochet hook
- Spare 5 mm / US 8, 60 cm / 24 in. long circular needle
- Tapestry needle
- Two 40.5 x 40.5 cm / 16 x 16 in. cushion pads

Continued on page 190

TENSION

19 sts and 26 rows = 10 cm /4 in. in St st
Be sure to check your tension.

NOTES

- These cushions are worked back and forth in rows, with the colour pattern worked as stranded colourwork. Certain sections are duplicate stitched after colourwork is complete. A provisional cast on is used so the beginning and last rows can be seamlessly joined using Kitchener stitch.

- If you don't want to work stranded colourwork back and forth and then add duplicate stitch details when the knitting is complete, you may want to use the intarsia technique to make these pillows, adding the extra details as you knit rather than embroidering them on afterwards.

PATTERN STITCH

Stocking Stitch (any number of sts)

Row 1 (RS): Knit.

Row 2 (WS): Purl.

Rep Rows 1 and 2 for patt.

CUSHION

R2-D2 ONLY

With CC1, CO 76 sts using Chained Provisional CO.

C-3PO ONLY

With MC, CO 76 sts using Chained Provisional CO.

BOTH CUSHIONS

Next row (RS): Purl.

Beg Chart A for R2-D2 cushion or Chart B for C-3PO cushion and work Rows 1–104.

Turn row (WS): With MC only, knit.

Cont in St st for 103 rows, or until back of cushion measures same as front to turn row. Do not cast off; leave sts on needle, or place on waste yarn.

Using duplicate st, add rem colour to front side according to chart.

FINISHING

Block lightly.

Remove provisional CO and place resulting 76 sts on spare cir needle.

With MC and RS facing, join sts from beg and end using Kitchener st.

Join one side edge using mattress st.

Weave in ends.

Insert cushion pad and join rem side edge using mattress st.

BEHIND THE SCENES:

C-3PO's design was inspired by the android from the black-and-white film *Metropolis* (1927). British actor Anthony Daniels, who portrays C-3PO in all nine films in the Skywalker Saga, gave him the personality of a neurotic British butler.

R2-D2's voice was created by sound designer Ben Burtt, who used a combination of his own voice and an ARP 2600 analog synthesizer.

CHART A

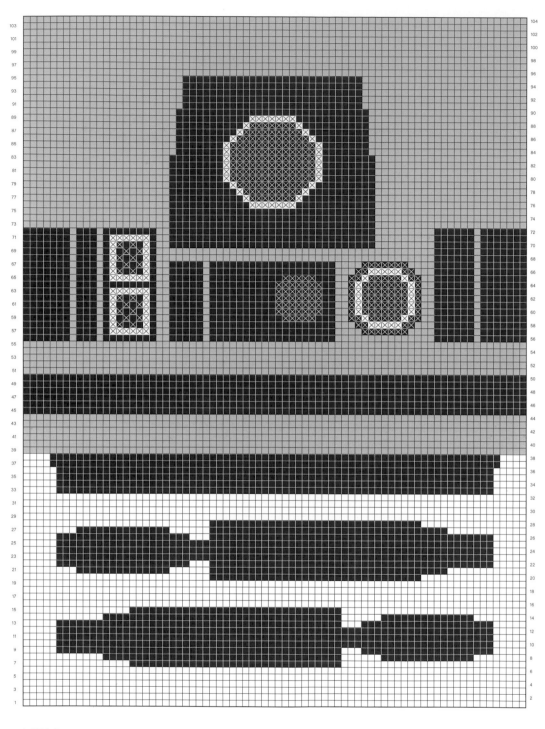

KEY

■ MC	■ CC3	⊠ work with MC or CC4, duplicate st with CC1
□ CC1	▨ CC4	⊠ work with MC, duplicate st with CC2
		⊠ work with MC or CC4, duplicate st with CC3

CHART B

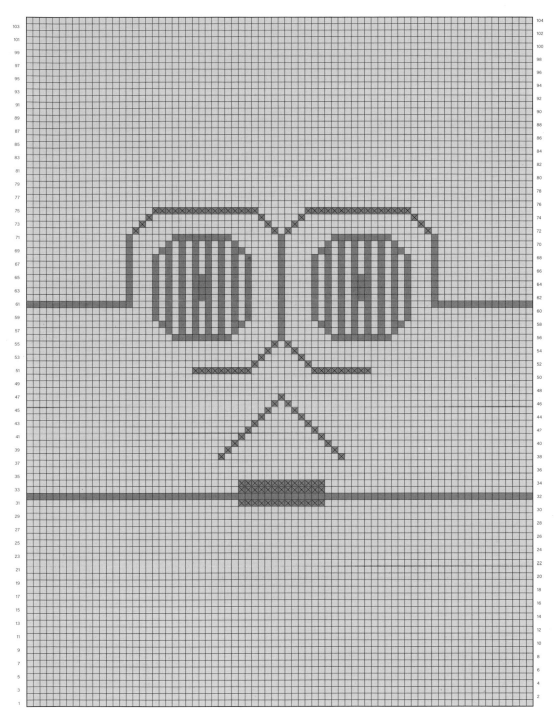

KEY

☐ MC

■ CC

☒ work with MC, duplicate st with CC

VILLAINOUS MINI SWEATER ORNAMENTS

Designed by: **CHRISTY HOUGHTON**

LEVEL:

Across nine epic saga films, *Star Wars* has given us some truly unforgettable villains. Darth Maul and his black facial tattoos, Darth Vader with his legendary ventilator mask, the iconic storm-trooper helmet, Kylo Ren's evil mask inspired by his grandfather's, fan favourite Boba Fett's durasteel armoured helmet – these symbols represent villains who are masters of inspiring fear and awe in the hearts of Galactic citizens. Now you can, too, by gifting one of these adorable mini sweater ornaments to the *Star Wars*–loving friend – or enemy – of your choosing.

These tiny pullover ornaments are all worked identically, with unique duplicate stitching added after the knitting. Worked from the top down with traditional raglan increasing, the body and sleeves are separated, then the body is worked in stocking stitch and edged with 1x1 ribbing. The sleeve stitches are then picked up and worked in the round. This quintet of baddies is perfect for gift toppers, ornaments or to hang in your cubicle as a reminder not to head towards the dark side.

SIZE
One size

FINISHED MEASUREMENTS
Chest: 16 cm / 6¼ in.
Length: 11.5 cm / 4½ in.

YARN
3-ply weight (super fine #1) yarn, shown in Yarn Café Creations *Biscotti Sock* (85% superwash merino wool, 15% nylon; 400 m / 437 yd per 100 g / 3½ oz. hank), 1 hank each

Colour A: Woodsmoke
Colour B: Pepper
Colour C: Twilight
Colour D: Cranberry
Colour E: Sunshine
Colour F: Mascara
Colour G: Bare
Colour H: Sand
Colour I: Basil
Colour J: White Pepper

COLOURWAYS
DARTH VADER:
Main Colour (MC): Woodsmoke (A)
Contrast Colour 1 (CC1): Mascara (F)
Contrast Colour 2 (CC2): Pepper (B)
Contrast Colour 3 (CC3): Bare (G)

DARTH MAUL:
Main Colour (MC): Pepper (B)
Contrast Colour 1 (CC1): Sunshine (E)
Contrast Colour 2 (CC2): Cranberry (D)
Contrast Colour 3 (CC3): Mascara (F)
Contrast Colour 4 (CC4): Sand (H)

STORMTROOPER:
Main Colour (MC): Twilight (C)
Contrast Colour 1 (CC1): Pepper (B)
Contrast Colour 2 (CC2): Mascara (F)
Contrast Colour 3 (CC3): Bare (G)

Continued on page 196

BOBA FETT:

Main Colour (MC): Cranberry (D)

Contrast Colour 1 (CC1): Basil (I)

Contrast Colour 2 (CC2): Woodsmoke (A)

Contrast Colour 3 (CC3): Sunshine (E)

Contrast Colour 4 (CC4): Mascara (F)

Contrast Colour 5 (CC5): White Pepper (J)

Contrast Colour 6 (CC6): Pepper (B)

KYLO REN:

Main Colour (MC): Sunshine (E)

Contrast Colour 1 (CC1): Cranberry (D)

Contrast Colour 2 (CC2): Mascara (F)

Contrast Colour 3 (CC3): Pepper (B)

NEEDLES

- 2.75 mm / US 2 set of 4 or 5 double-pointed needles or 60–80 cm / 24–32 in. long circular needle for Magic Loop method or size needed to obtain tension

NOTIONS

- Stitch markers
- Stitch holder or waste yarn
- Tapestry needle

TENSION

30 sts and 44 rnds = 10 cm / 4 in. in St st.
Make sure to check your tension.

NOTES

- These sweaters are worked in the round from the top down. The villain is added using duplicate stitch embroidery once the sweater is complete.

PATTERN STITCHES

Stocking Stitch (any number of sts)
All rnds: Knit.

K1, P1 Rib (multiple of 2 sts)
All rnds: *K1, p1; rep from * to end of rnd.

YOKE

With MC, CO 26 sts. Pm and join to work in the rnd, being careful not to twist sts.

Work 4 rnds in K1, P1 Rib.

Setup rnd: K4 for sleeve, pm, k9 for front, pm, k4 for sleeve, pm, then k9 for back.

Inc rnd: *K1, M1L, knit to 1 st before marker, M1R, k1; rep from * 3 more times – 8 sts inc'd.

Next rnd: Knit.

Rep last 2 rnds 5 more times – 74 sts, with 16 sts for each sleeve and 21 sts each for front and back.

Ind rnd: *Knit to marker, sm, k1, M1L, knit to 1 st before marker, M1R, k1; rep from * once more – 78 sts, with 16 sts for each sleeve and 23 sts each for front and back.

DIVIDE BODY AND SLEEVES

Next rnd: Place first 16 sts on holder or waste yarn for sleeve, sm, knit to next marker, remove marker, place next 16 sts on holder or waste yarn for sleeve, sm, knit to end of rnd – 46 sts rem.

BODY

Work even in St st for 27 rnds.
Work 3 rnds in K1, P1 Rib.
Cast off all sts loosely in patt.

SLEEVES

Place 16 sleeve sts on dpn. Pm and join to work in the rnd.

Rnd 1: Knit.

Dec rnd: K1, ssk, knit to last 3 sts, k2tog, k1 – 2 sts dec'd.

Rep Dec rnd every 7 rnds twice more – 10 sts rem.

Work 3 rnds in K1, P1 Rib.
Cast off all sts loosely in patt.

FINISHING

Weave in ends. Block as desired.

Mark centre of front using waste yarn to run a line of tacking sts from bottom edge to neck edge. Using colours for your chosen chart, centring patt on the front of the sweater and just above ribbing, embroider the face using duplicate st. *Note:* Any squares on the chart showing the main colour of the sweater are not embroidered; leave those stitches in the main colour and uncovered by duplicate st.

'I FIND YOUR LACK OF FAITH DISTURBING.'

– DARTH VADER, *STAR WARS*: EPISODE IV *A NEW HOPE*

BOBA FETT CHART

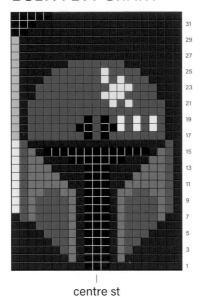

31
29
27
25
23
21
19
17
15
13
11
9
7
5
3
1

centre st

DARTH MAUL CHART

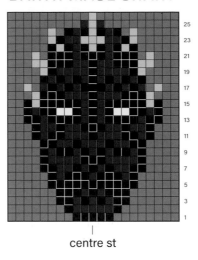

25
23
21
19
17
15
13
11
9
7
5
3
1

centre st

KEY

A
B
C
D
E
F
G
H
I
J

DARTH VADER CHART

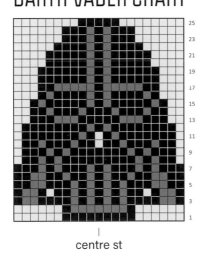

25
23
21
19
17
15
13
11
9
7
5
3
1

centre st

KYLO REN CHART

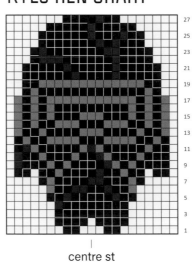

27
25
23
21
19
17
15
13
11
9
7
5
3
1

centre st

STORM TROOPER CHART

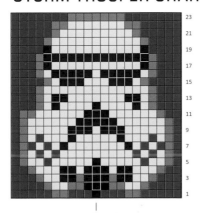

23
21
19
17
15
13
11
9
7
5
3
1

centre st

TECHNIQUES

CAST ONS

BACKWARD LOOP CAST ON

*Holding the yarn over your left thumb with the end coming from the ball between your last three fingers and at the outside of the thumb, insert the needle up under the yarn next to the outside of your thumb. Remove your thumb from the loop and pull the end to tighten the yarn slightly on the needle. Repeat from * until the required number of stitches has been cast on.

CABLE CAST ON

Make a slipknot and place it on the needle. Holding the needle with the slipknot in your left hand, insert the right needle into the stitch and knit, but do not slip the stitch from the left needle. Place this new stitch on the left needle. *Insert the right needle between the first two stitches on the left needle and knit, then place the new stitch on the left needle. Repeat from * until the required number of stitches are on the needle.

LONG TAIL CAST ON

Make a slipknot with the yarn, leaving a tail long enough to cast on the required number of stitches (usually about 2.5 cm / 1 in. per stitch) and place the slipknot on the needle. Holding the needle in your right hand, clasp both strands in your lower three fingers with the long tail over your thumb and the end coming from the ball over your index finger.

*Spread your thumb and index finger apart to form a V.

Insert the needle tip up between the two strands on your thumb. Bring the needle tip over the top of the first strand around your index finger, then down to draw a loop between the strands on your thumb. Remove your thumb and tighten the stitch on the needle – 1 stitch cast on. Place your thumb and index finger between the strands of yarn again. Repeat from * until the required number of stitches has been cast on.

TWISTED GERMAN CAST ON

Make a slipknot and place it on the needle. *Holding the needle and yarn as for a Long Tail Cast On, bring the needle towards you, under the strands around your thumb. Swing the tip up and towards you again, then down into the loop on your thumb and up in front of the loop on your thumb. Then swing it over the top of the loops and over the first strand on your index finger, catch that strand, and bring the needle back down through the thumb loop and to the front, turning your thumb as needed to make room for the needle to pass through. Remove your thumb from the loop, then pull the strands to tighten the stitch. Repeat from * until the required number of stitches has been cast on.

PROVISIONAL CAST ONS

With a crochet hook and waste yarn, make a chain a few stitches longer than the number needed to begin knitting. Cut the waste yarn

and fasten off the remaining stitch, making sure you do not tighten the last stitch too much.

With the working yarn, begin a couple of chains from one end. *Insert the needle into the back bump of the next chain, wrap the yarn around the needle and draw through a loop – 1 stitch cast on. Repeat from * until the required number of stitches are on the needle and at least one or two chains remain at the end of the pick-up.

When finishing the edge or picking up the stitches to continue working in the other direction, pull the waste yarn tail out of the last stitch cast on and pull carefully to unzip the edge, placing the resulting stitches on the needle.

MAGIC LOOP

This is an alternative to DPNs or working with 2 circular needles for small circumference knitting. With a 32" (80 cm) or 40" (102 cm) circular knitting needle, cast on the amount of stitches called for in the pattern.

Divide the stitches in half evenly by bending the needle cord in half and sliding stitches to each needle tip keeping them parallel, being careful not to twist stitches. A loop of cord will form on the left side. The working yarn should always be coming off of the back needle.

Push the front or left-hand needle stitches to the needle tip, then pull the back or right-hand needle out to form a loop of cord on the right side. There are now two equal loops of cord coming out of both sides of the casted on stitches.

Work across the front half stitches, being mindful to bring the needle under the yarn when starting so as not to create an extra stitch when drawing up the yarn.

When the left-hand needle stitches are worked turn work 180 degrees, slide the unworked back stitches to the tip of the needle (this is now the front needle) and pull the empty needle tip out to create a new loop on the opposite side, centering just-worked stitches on the back needle.

Work across as before. Continue in this manner according to pattern instructions.

INCREASES

K1f&b: Knit into the front of the next stitch but do not remove it from the left-hand needle. Bring the right needle to the back of the work and knit into the back of the same stitch, then slip the stitch from the left needle – 1 stitch increased.

M1/M1L (make 1/make 1 left leaning): Insert the left needle under the strand between the stitch just worked and the next stitch, from front to back, then knit through the back loop – 1 stitch increased.

M1P (make 1 purlwise): Insert the right needle under the strand between the stitch just worked and the next stitch, from front to back, then purl through the back loop – 1 stitch increased.

M1R (make 1 right leaning): Insert the left needle under the

strand between the stitch just worked and the next stitch, from back to front, then knit through the front loop – 1 stitch increased.

LLI (left lifted increase): Insert the left needle into the back of the stitch *below* the last stitch worked on the right needle, then knit this stitch – 1 stitch increased.

RLI (right lifted increase): Insert the right needle into the front of the stitch *below* the next stitch to be worked on the left needle, then knit this stitch – 1 stitch increased.

SHORT ROWS
WRAP AND TURN (W&T) SHORT ROWS
On knit rows: Knit to the stitch before wrapping. With the yarn at the back of the work, slip the next stitch purlwise to the right needle, bring the yarn to the front between the needles, slip the stitch back to the left needle and bring the yarn back between the needles to the purl side. Turn the work.

On purl rows: Purl to the stitch before wrapping. With the yarn at the front of the work, slip the next stitch purlwise to the right needle, bring the yarn to the back between the needles, slip the stitch back to the left needle and bring the yarn to the front between needles to the purl side. Turn the work.

To hide the wrap on a subsequent row: Work to the wrapped stitch, pick up the wrap from front to back for a knit stitch (and from back to front for a purl stitch) and place the wrap on the left needle. Work the wrap together with the stitch.

GERMAN SHORT ROWS
Work to the turning point, then turn the work.

Slip the first stitch purlwise with the yarn at the front of the work, from the left needle to the right needle. Pull the yarn tightly up and over the top of the right needle so that both legs of the slipped stitch are pulled over the top of the needle, creating a double stitch (DS). If the next stitch is a purl stitch, bring the yarn back to the front between the needles. If the next stitch is a knit stitch, keep the yarn at the back of the work.

To work the DS, on the next knit or purl row, knit or purl *both* legs of the DS together.

COLOUR WORK
INTARSIA
Intarsia is a way of adding isolated blocks of colours within a knitted piece without stranding the unused colour across the back of the work. Yarns are interlocked on the wrong side when changing colours to prevent holes from appearing in the finished knitting.

Before you begin to knit, wind off yarn for each section of colour to be worked, winding small amounts around yarn bobbins. For very small areas, simply cut the yarn to the length you'll need. Cut a separate length of yarn for each section of colour, adding about 15 cm / 6 in. at each end for weaving in the ends.

When adding a new colour, you'll also have to add another length of yarn for the colour on the other side of the new colour.

To join a new yarn, drop the yarn you've just worked with, then knit or purl the next stitch with the new yarn, making sure to leave a tail about 15 cm / 6 in. 6 in. long. Work to the next colour change.

To change colours with yarns already in the work, knit or purl to the point where colours will change, bring the new colour up from underneath the strand of the colour being dropped, then begin working with the new colour. Make sure you adjust the tension if needed so that the last stitch worked with that colour on the previous row will look the same as the other stitches.

It's advisable to weave in ends after knitting is finished; if you weave in ends while you are knitting, any high-contrast values (such as black and white) will show through on the right side. After threading the tail onto a tapestry needle, adjust the tension of the first (or last) stitch if needed, knot the tail to a stitch of the same colour, then weave the tail in the backs of stitches of the same colour if possible, or through the interlocking join between colours.

STRANDED COLOURWORK
Usually referred to as Fair Isle knitting, stranded colourwork uses two colours per round, with the colour not currently being used stranded loosely across the wrong side. Both yarns can be held in either the right or left hand, however you prefer to knit, or with one colour in each hand. Whichever method you use, make sure you maintain even tension. When rounds of stranded colourwork are placed between rounds of stocking stitch, check both tensions before you begin; most knitters will knit the stranded colourwork section more tightly than plain stocking stitch. If this describes you, adjust your needle size when switching to the stranded section, and remember to change back to the smaller needle(s) when beginning the next section of plain stocking stitch.

As you work across a round of the pattern, spread the stitches just worked apart slightly before knitting the next stitch with the colour that has been floated across the wrong side. The float across the back should be relaxed, not sagging or pulling.

If floats between colour changes will be more than 1.3–2 cm / ½–¾ in. long, it's a good idea to weave in the unused colour to reduce the risk of snagging the float later. The easiest way to do this is to hold the colour to be woven in your left hand and the working colour in your right hand. Insert the right needle into the next stitch and *under* the floated yarn, then knit as usual, allowing the floated yarn to come back down behind the needles so that the working yarn will lie over the top of it on the next stitch. If you weave in the floated colour every other stitch, that uses more yarn than weaving in every few stitches and can create a stiff fabric.

DUPLICATE STITCH
Sometimes called Swiss darning, duplicate stitch is a way of adding sections of colour to a knitted piece without having to work stranded

knitting or intarsia. The technique covers each stitch completely. Large areas can become thick and stiff, so it's best used in small areas.

With the colour to be stitched threaded into a tapestry needle, insert the needle from wrong side to right side in the stitch *below* the first stitch to be covered. *Insert the tapestry needle under both legs of the stitch in the row *above* the stitch to be covered and pull the yarn through, being careful not to pull the yarn too tightly. Insert the needle back into the same spot where you initially brought it to the right side and pull the yarn through to completely cover the first stitch. Bring the needle up through the stitch below the next stitch to be covered. Repeat from * to continue covering stitches.

SEAMING TECHNIQUES
KITCHENER STITCH

Sometimes also called grafting, Kitchener stitch joins two sets of live stitches without a visible seam. This seaming method is not well suited for joining shoulder seams, which need to support the weight of the body and sleeves of the garment. This should be used for smaller seamed areas, or for joining sections of a scarf or shawl that is expected to be stretched.

Work a few stitches at a time, pulling the yarn loosely, then adjust the length of each stitch to match the tension on each side of the join.

Place each set of stitches to be joined on separate needles, making sure the needle tips are at the right-hand edge.

Hold both needles in your left hand, with the needle tips pointing to the right.

Step 1: Insert tapestry needle purlwise through first stitch on front needle and pull the yarn through, leaving stitch on front needle.

Step 2: Insert tapestry needle knitwise through first stitch on back needle and pull the yarn through, leaving stitch on back needle.

Step 3: Insert tapestry needle knitwise through first stitch on front needle, slip stitch from front needle and pull the yarn through.

Step 4: Insert tapestry needle purlwise through next stitch on front needle and pull the yarn through, leaving stitch on front needle.

Step 5: Insert tapestry needle purlwise through first stitch on back needle, slip stitch from back needle and pull the yarn through.

Step 6: Insert tapestry needle knitwise through next stitch on back needle and pull the yarn through, leaving stitch on back needle.

Repeat Steps 3–6 until the yarn has been threaded through the last stitch of each needle once. Insert tapestry needle knitwise into last stitch on front needle, slip stitch from needle and pull yarn through. Then insert tapestry needle knitwise into last stitch on back needle, slip stitch from needle and pull yarn through. Fasten off on the wrong side.

MATTRESS STITCH

Mattress stitch creates an invisible seam along vertical edges.

Place the pieces being sewn together side by side on a flat surface, with the right sides facing you. Thread a piece of yarn about three times longer than the seam to be sewn into a tapestry needle.

Beginning at the bottom edge, insert the tapestry needle under one bar between the edge stitches on one piece, then under the corresponding bar on the other piece. *Insert the tapestry needle under the next two bars of the first piece, then under the next two bars on the other piece. Repeat from *, alternating sides until the seam is complete, ending on the last bar or pairs of bars on the first piece. Fasten off on the wrong side.

THREE-NEEDLE CAST OFF

The three-needle cast off is a way of joining two sets of live stitches in a cast-off edge, creating a firm seam. This method of seaming is ideal for seams that need firmness, such as a shoulder seam that supports the weight of the body and sleeves of a garment.

Place each set of stitches to be joined on separate needles, making sure the needle tips are at the right-hand edge.

Hold both needles in your left hand, with the needle tips pointing to the right.

Insert the right needle knitwise into the first stitch on both needles, then knit them together – 1 stitch from each needle has been joined. *Knit the next stitch on both needles together, lift the first stitch worked over the stitch just worked and off the needle – 1 stitch cast off. Repeat from * until all stitches have been worked and 1 stitch remains on the right needle. Cut the yarn and fasten off the remaining stitch.

WET BLOCKING

Wet blocking is a finishing method often used to block items knit in lace or stranded colourwork; for lace it allows the work to be stretched to open up the stitches, and for stranded colourwork it helps to even out the knitting tension for a more uniform appearance. It can be used for pieces knit using other techniques as well, and most natural fibres block well using this method. There are two options for wet blocking an item: Submerge the entire piece in water before pinning it out to shape, or pin the item to shape and spray it with water to dampen it.

If you choose to submerge the piece in water, place the finished knitting in a tub or sink of cool water, adding a no-rinse wash to the water if desired. Make sure the item is thoroughly wet; a long soak time is not required. Carefully remove the piece from the tub and squeeze to remove excess water, making sure you do not wring the work. Lay the piece on a dry towel and roll up the towel. Either place the towel on the floor and walk over it a few times, or spin in a washing machine (spin cycle only) to remove more excess water. Unroll the towel and remove the piece, then lay it out to dry completely away from sunlight or a heat source, pinning if needed.

Take care when blocking knits that have dark and light colours together, especially reds, as these colours may bleed into the lighter areas.

ABBREVIATIONS

approx	approximately
beg	begin(ning)(s)
CC	contrast colour
cir	circular
cm	centimetre(s)
cn	cable needle
CO	cast on
cont	continu(e)(ing)
dec('d)	decreas(es)(ed)(ing)
dpn	double-pointed needle(s)
DS	double stitch
g	gram(s)
in.	inch(es)
inc('d)	increas(es)(ed)(ing)
k	knit
k1f&b	knit into the front and back of the same stitch
k2tog	knit 2 stitches together (1 stitch decreased)
k2tog-tbl	knit 2 stitches together through the back loops (1 stitch decreased)
k3tog	knit 3 stitches together (2 stitches decreased)
kwise	knitwise (as if to knit)
LH	left-hand
LLI	left lifted increase
m	metre(s)
M1	make 1 stitch
M1L	make 1 stitch, left leaning
M1P	make 1 stitch purlwise
M1R	make 1 stitch, right leaning
MC	main colour
mm	millimeter(s)
oz	ounce(s)
p	purl
p2tog	purl 2 stitches together (1 stitch decreased)
p2tog-tbl	purl 2 stitches together through the back loops (1 stitch decreased)
patt	pattern(s)

pm	place marker
pwise	purlwise (as if to purl)
rem	remain(s)(ing)
rep	repeat(s)
RH	right-hand
RLI	right lifted increase
rnd(s)	round(s)
RS	right side
s2kp	slip 2 stitches together knitwise, knit 1, then pass slipped stitches over (2 stitches decreased)
sl	slip
sm	slip marker
ssk	slip, slip, knit: slip 2 stitches knitwise, one at a time, insert left needle into front loop of both stitches, and knit them together through the back loops (1 stitch decreased)
ssp	slip, slip, purl: slip 2 stitches knitwise, one at a time, return stitches to the left needle in their turned position, then purl them together through the back loops (1 stitch decreased)
St st	stocking stitch
st(s)	stitch(es)
tbl	through the back loop(s)
tog	together
w&t	wrap and turn
WS	wrong side
wyib	with yarn held at the back of the work
wyif	with yarn held at the front of the work
yd	yards
yo	yarn over
[ ]	used to indicate instructions to be repeated
( )	used for instructions for additional sizes
/	used to separate metric measurements from inches, with additional sizes in brackets ( )
*	used to indicate the beginning of a length of instructions to be repeated

YARN SUBSTITUTION

All of the patterns in this book list the exact yarns used to create the project. If, however, you are unable to source the yarn listed, it is possible to find substitutions by searching for them online – www.yarbsub.com is a useful resource. Alternatively, you can find substitute yarns yourself. First, you will need to identify the thickness of the original yarn. The best way to ascertain this is to check the tension instruction at the beginning of every pattern. Opposite is a yarn weight conversion table that will help with finding the right weight. Note that the yarns listed in the projects use UK weight terms. Additionally, look for a yarn with a similar fibre content. Then knit a tension swatch with your chosen yarn to make sure you use the right needles. Lastly, to make sure you have the right amount of yarn, multiply the length of original yarn by the amount of balls listed. Then divide this figure by the number of metres/yards stated on the substituted yarn, which will give you the number of balls you need.

YARN WEIGHT CONVERSION*

UK	US
SUPER CHUNKY	SUPER BULKY
CHUNKY	BULKY
ARAN	WORSTED
DK	DK
4 PLY	SPORT/FINGERING
3 PLY	FINGERING
LACE	LACE

*THESE ARE APPROXIMATE WEIGHTS

YARN RESOURCE GUIDE

ANZULA LUXURY FIBERS
WWW.ANZULA.COM

BERROCO
WWW.BERROCO.COM

BLUE SKY FIBERS
WWW.BLUESKYFIBERS.COM

BROOKLYN TWEED
WWW.BROOKLYNTWEED.COM

CASCADE YARNS
WWW.CASCADEYARNS.COM

DI GILPIN
WWW.DIGILPIN.COM

DRAGON HOARD YARN
WWW.DRAGONHOARDYARNCO.COM

EMMA'S YARN
WWW.EMMASYARN.COM

THE FIBERISTS
WWW.THEFIBERISTS.COM

FREIA FINE HANDPAINTS
WWW.FREIAFIBERS.COM

HAZEL KNITS
WWW.HAZELKNITS.COM

KATIA/KFI
WWW.KNITTINGFEVER.COM

KELBOURNE WOOLENS
WWW.KELBOURNEWOOLENS.COM

KIM DYES YARN
WWW.KIMDYESYARN.COM

THE LEMONADE SHOP
WWW.THELEMONADESHOPYARNS.COM

LOLABEAN YARN CO.
WWW.LOLABEANYARNCO.COM

MISS BABS
WWW.MISSBABS.COM

NEIGHBORHOOD FIBER CO.
WWW.NEIGHBORHOODFIBERCO.COM

OINK PIGMENTS
WWW.OINKPIGMENTS.COM

PLYMOUTH YARN
WWW.PLYMOUTHYARN.COM

QUEEN CITY YARN
WWW.QUEENCITYYARN.COM

QUINCE & CO.
WWW.QUINCEANDCO.COM

ROWAN
WWW.KNITROWAN.COM

SWEETGEORGIA YARNS
WWW.SWEETGEORGIAYARNS.COM

URBAN GIRL YARNS
WWW.URBANGIRLYARNS.COM

YARN CAFÉ CREATIONS
WWW.YARNCAFECREATIONS.COM

FOR CALLUM. MAY THE FORCE BE WITH YOU, ALWAYS.

ACKNOWLEDGEMENTS

There is simply no way I could have made this book in less than twelve parsecs without my fearless editor. Hilary-Wan Kenobi, there's no one else I'd want to travel at lightspeed with.

The Force is strong in my family. Roger, Callum and Astrid: There is no better bunch of scruffy-looking nerf herders this side of the Death Star. Thank you for letting me bounce ideas off you, talk nonstop about *Star Wars* and nerd out. Thank you for watching the films over and over with me. There may have been times you wanted to put me in carbonite, but there is no one else I'd want to travel to a galaxy far, far away with.

I am the luckiest person in the universe to be in the company of such gifted and inventive knitters. Thank you to the talented designers for making this collection out of this world. Your hard work, dedication and ability to put up with my *Star Wars* jokes made me excited to work on this book each day. I am honoured to be in your company.

Much appreciation to Therese Chynoweth for her Jedi-like tech editing skills. Thank you for not turning to the dark side.

To brilliant sample knitters Drew Harder, Kathey Harris, Jane Stanley and Marta Poling, you're better than any protocol droid. Many thanks for your skills.

Gratitude to the yarn dyers and yarn companies who provided yarn support. Yoda best.

To the outstanding folks at Insight, I am thrilled to be making another book with you. Thank you for flying through this galaxy with me and making me look good. Let's hit Tosche Station to pick up those power converters next time I'm in town.

PAVILION

First published in the United Kingdom by
Pavilion
43 Great Ormond Street
London
WC1N 3HZ

Library of Congress Cataloging-in-Publication Data available.

Published by arrangement with Insight Editions, LP, 800 A Street, San Rafael, CA 94901, USA, www.insighteditions.com

ISBN: 978-1-91166-357-7

A CIP catalogue record for this book is available from the British Library

10 9 8 7 6 5 4 3 2 1

Publisher: Raoul Goff
VP of Licensing and Partnerships: Vanessa Lopez
VP of Creative: Chrissy Kwasnik
VP of Manufacturing: Alix Nicholaeff
Designer: Judy Wiatrek Trum
Editor: Hilary VandenBroek
Editorial Assistants: Anna Wostenberg and Harrison Tunggal
Managing Editor: Lauren LePera
Production Editor: Jennifer Bentham
Senior Production Manager, Subsidiary Rights: Lina s Palma
Production Manager: Eden Orlesky
Anglicisation: Sarah Hoggett

FOR LUCASFILM:

Senior Editor: Robert Simpson
Creative Director: Michael Siglain
Art Director: Troy Alders
Asset Management: Chris Argyopoulos, Nicole LaCoursiere, Gabrielle Levenson,
Bryce Pinkos, Erik Sanchez, and Sarah Williams
Lucasfilm Story Group: Kelsey Sharpe, Emily Shkoukani, and Kate Izquierdo
Lucasfilm Art Department: Phil Szostak

Technical Editor: Therese Chynoweth
Photography by Tyler Chartier
Prop Styling by Caroline Hall and Elena Craig
Hair and Makeup by Chris McDonald

Thank you to our models: Amy, Autumn, Caroline, Karina, Esme, Elena, Josephine,
Courtney, George, Jaya, Opal, Emi, Ray, Violet, Annabelle, and Lukas

ROOTS of PEACE   REPLANTED PAPER

Pavilion, in association with Roots of Peace, will plant two trees for each tree used in the manufacturing
of this book. Roots of Peace is an internationally renowned humanitarian organization dedicated to
eradicating land mines worldwide and converting war-torn lands into productive farms and wildlife
habitats. Roots of Peace will plant two million fruit and nut trees in Afghanistan and provide
farmers there with the skills and support necessary for sustainable land use.

Printed and bound in China by Insight editions
www.pavilionbooks.com